北大版对外汉语教材·公共选修课系列

学唱中国歌

于鹏 焦毓梅 编著

刘甦 翻译

Angela Lee（李文睿） 校译

图书在版编目(CIP)数据

学唱中国歌 / 于鹏, 焦毓梅编著; 刘甦翻译. —北京: 北京大学出版社, 2009.1
(北大版对外汉语教材·公共选修课系列)
ISBN 978-7-301-14730-6

Ⅰ.学… Ⅱ.①于… ②焦… ③刘… Ⅲ.汉语—对外汉语教学—教材 Ⅳ.H195.4

中国版本图书馆 CIP 数据核字(2008)第 191116 号

书　　　名:	学唱中国歌
著作责任者:	于鹏　焦毓梅　编著　刘甦　翻译
责 任 编 辑:	沈　岚
标 准 书 号:	ISBN 978-7-301-14730-6/H·2174
出 版 发 行:	北京大学出版社
地　　　址:	北京市海淀区成府路 205 号　100871
网　　　址:	http://www.pup.cn
电　　　话:	邮购部 62752015　发行部 62750672　编辑部 62753374　出版部 62754962
电 子 邮 箱:	zpup@pup.pku.edu.cn
印　刷　者:	北京大学印刷厂
经　销　者:	新华书店
	787 毫米×1092 毫米　16 开本　9.75 印张　240 千字
	2009 年 1 月第 1 版　2017 年 5 月第 3 次印刷
定　　　价:	38.00 元(含 1 张 CD)

未经许可,不得以任何方式复制或抄袭本书之部分或全部内容。
版权所有,侵权必究　举报电话: 010-62752024
电子邮箱: fd@pup.pku.edu.cn

学唱中国歌

前 言

  歌曲是最大众化的音乐形式,它常常具有地域性特点。不同国家、不同民族地区的歌曲往往具有鲜明的民族特色和地方色彩,有时某一特定的旋律和唱腔会与某一特定地区紧密联系在一起,甚至成为这一地区的显著性标志之一。歌曲又是世界性的,有时一首歌会跨越国界,在世界范围内广为传唱,当不同国家、不同种族、操着不同语言的人同唱一首歌的时候,音乐成为了共同的语言,把他们的心紧紧地连在了一起。

  本书精选19首中国歌曲,每首独立成篇。这些歌曲可分为三部分:一是以《茉莉花》、《达坂城的姑娘》、《月儿弯弯照九州》等为代表的优秀民歌。二是以《祝你生日快乐》、《找朋友》等为代表的优秀儿歌,满足幼儿或汉语初学者学唱的需要。三是以《常回家看看》、《爱情鸟》、《阳光总在风雨后》等为代表的当代流行歌曲。

  在歌曲的选编中,作者综合考虑了词语的难易度、作品对现实生活的反应、欣赏性、词曲作者及歌手的影响、中国传统文化等因素。歌曲内容包括爱情、亲情、风物、景观等多个主题,力求寓教于乐,使留学生在歌声中学习汉语,从而进一步了解中国文化,走进中国人的生活。

  这本书得以问世,应该感谢北京大学出版社的沈岚老师的大力支持,她在本书的编写过程中提出了很多宝贵的修改意见,我的韩国好友郑安修和金荣振友情听录了本书十余首歌曲的五线谱,并审定了全书的乐谱,在此一并表示谢意。

于鹏　焦毓梅
2008.5

Foreword

Songs, as the most popular form of music, vary greatly in style due to geographical differences. Songs of different countries and ethnic groups often take on special ethnic and regional characteristics. Some forms of singing and some special melodies may represent a certain region and be the symbol of that part of the world. Music is also the common language of the whole world. Sometimes a song may cross borders and nations to be sung by people from different countries and ethnic backgrounds, who speak different languages. In this way, people's hearts can come together through music.

This book has selected 20 Chinese songs, each in one separate chapter, which fall generally into three categories: folk songs (like "Jasmine", "The Girl from Dabancheng", and "Crescent Moon over China"); children's songs (like "Happy Birthday to You" and "Looking for a Friend") to cater to the needs of children and beginners; and contemporary popular songs (like "Come Back Home Often", "Love Bird", and "After Storms There Always Comes Sunshine").

The editors of this book have also taken into consideration factors like the difficulty of the language, the ideas conveyed by the song, its reflection of real life, its aesthetic value, the influence of the song-writer and singer, and how related it is to Chinese traditional culture, etc. The songs are about common themes like love, family, scenery and landscapes, etc. The book tries its best to teach people something about the language while having fun, and help students learn Chinese when singing songs, so they know more about Chinese culture and better understand to Chinese life.

We would also like to express our sincere gratitude to Shen Lan of Peking University Press, who generously offered many suggestions for the book. Without her help this book could not possibly be what you see today. Our heart-felt thankfulness also goes to our great Korean friends, Jeong Ahn Soo and Kim Young Jin, who kindly helped record in musical notations over half of the selected songs and revised the rest of the music sheets.

Yu Peng, Jiao Yumei
May, 2008

学唱中国歌

目 录
Contents

1 祝你生日快乐 ·································· 1
  Happy Birthday to You
2 找朋友 ··· 6
  Looking for a Friend
3 天堂 ·· 10
  Heaven
4 掀起了你的盖头来 ························· 15
  Lift Your Veil
5 达坂城的姑娘 ······························· 21
  The Girl from Dabancheng
6 月儿弯弯照九州 ····························· 27
  Crescent Moon over China
7 茉莉花 ··· 33
  Jasmine
8 爱情鸟 ··· 39
  Love Bird
9 糊涂的爱 ······································ 46
  Muddled Love
10 弯弯的月亮 ································· 54
   The Crescent Moon
11 常回家看看 ································· 62
   Come Back Home Often
12 青藏高原 ···································· 70
   Tibetan Plateau

学唱中国歌

13　雾里看花 ·················· 77
　　Flower in Mist

14　阳光总在风雨后 ·················· 84
　　After Storms There Always Comes Sunshine

15　一剪梅 ·················· 92
　　A Spray of Plum Blossom

16　心太软 ·················· 99
　　Too Soft a Heart

17　回娘家 ·················· 110
　　Going Back to My Parents' Home

18　送别 ·················· 120
　　A Valediction

19　说唱脸谱 ·················· 127
　　Rap Painting Mask

Vocabulary ·················· 141

学唱中国歌

1 祝你生日快乐
Happy Birthday to You

一 推荐絮语 (Introduction)

《祝你生日快乐》是世界上最广为传唱的歌曲之一，翻译成多国语言，跨越了种族和国界。这首歌曲原名 Good Morning to All（《大家早上好》），由美国的希尔姐妹创作于1893年。在1910—1930年间，有人将 Good Morning to All 配上新的歌词，改成了现在的 Happy Birthday to You（《祝你生日快乐》）。

Happy Birthday to You sits at the top of the list of "the most popular songs of the world". It has been translated into many different languages, and crossed the boundaries of nationality and culture. It comes from the song Good Morning to All written by the American sisters Meldred Hill and Patty Hill in 1893. The combination of the melody and the current lyrics appeared in the 1910s or 1920s.

二 歌词对读 (Chinese and English lyrics)

zhù nǐ shēng rì kuài lè
祝你生日快乐， Happy birthday to you,

zhù nǐ shēng rì kuài lè
祝你生日快乐， Happy birthday to you,

zhù nǐ shēng rì kuài lè
祝你生日快乐， Happy birthday to you,

学唱中国歌

<zhù nǐ shēng rì kuài lè>
祝你生日快乐！   Happy birthday to you!

三 生词详解 (New words)

1. 祝   (动)   zhù   wish; express good wishes
2. 你   (代)   nǐ   you
3. 生日 (名)   shēngrì   birthday
4. 快乐 (形)   kuàilè   happy

四 歌曲欣赏 (Music sheet)

祝你生日快乐

学唱中国歌

五 读一读 (Read the Following Passage)

面 条 Noodle

庆祝生日是世界性的文化习俗,但由于各国在文化传统和宗教信仰等方面的不同,人们在庆祝方式上不完全相同。在中国的大部分地方,人们在过生日时,常常要吃面条。

过生日时为什么要吃面条呢?因为面条又长又瘦("瘦"是指面薄而窄),"长瘦"与"长寿"同音,含有祝福人长命百岁的意思。过生日吃的面条,被称为长寿面。

"面条"这一名称最早出现于宋朝(960—1279)。那时面条的吃法就已经有很多种,除了煮之外,还有炒、焖、煎等,各种荤菜、素菜都可以用来拌面,吃法和现在已经差不多了。面条在宋朝时已经成为祝福新生儿长命百岁的象征了。这种习俗延续至今,长寿面就成了人们生日之餐的必备品。

The celebration of birthdays is a custom practiced worldwide. But due to differences in cultural traditions and religious beliefs, people's ways of celebration vary greatly. In major parts of China, people eat noodles for birthdays.

Why do they do that? Simply because noodles are long (*chang*) and thin (*shou*), and *changshou*, in Chinese, also means "longevity". Eating noodles expresses people's wish for long life. The noodles people eat for their birthday is called "*changshoumian* (longevity noodles)".

The Chinese word for noodle first became part of the common vocabulary in the Song Dynasty (960−1279 A.D.). Even back then there have been many ways of cooking noodles (boiling, stir-frying, stewing, frying, etc.), and any dishes (vegetarian or non-vegetarian) could be served with them, which is more or less the way they are served today. And from the Song Dynasty, noodles were used to wish new-born babies long life. This custom is still practiced today, with noodles as necessary for a birthday meal.

六 说一说 (Ask and Answer)

1. 在你的国家,人们过生日时吃什么?
2. 中国人过生日时为什么吃面条?
3. 说一说你最难忘的生日晚会。

七 做一做 (Tasks)

1. 参加朋友的生日晚会时,用汉语演唱《祝你生日快乐》。
2. 参考中国人的习惯,为自己、家人或朋友准备一个中西合璧的生日晚会。

八 词语链接 (Related Words or Phrases)

1. 面条	(名)	miàntiáo	noodles
2. 庆祝	(动)	qìngzhù	celebrate
3. 习俗	(名)	xísú	coustom
4. 长寿	(形)	chángshòu	long life, longevity
5. 蛋糕	(名)	dàngāo	cake
6. 点	(动)	diǎn	light; burn

学唱中国歌

7. 蜡烛　　　（名）　　làzhú　　　　candle
8. 许愿　　　　　　　　xǔ yuàn　　　make a wish
9. 吹　　　　（动）　　chuī　　　　 blow; puff
10. 祝福　　　（动）　　zhùfú　　　　wish; happiness

学唱中国歌

2 找朋友
Looking for a Friend

一 推荐絮语 (Introduction)

在中国,《找朋友》是一首广为传唱的儿童游戏歌曲。歌曲寓教于乐,使孩子在歌唱中学习与小伙伴友好相处。这首歌虽然是儿歌,具有内容简单、句式短小、简洁明快、朗朗上口的特点,但唱出的却不只是儿童的心声,因为生活中离不了朋友,不管是孩子还是成人。

In China, "Looking for a Friend" is a popular song sung in children's games. Adding fun to education, this song teaches kids to be friendly to others. Although this is a child's song with simple and brief lyrics, it has a delightful rhythm and is very catchy. It expresses more than just the hearts of children, because we all need friends, whether we are kids or adults.

二 歌词对读 (Chinese and English lyrics)

zhǎo ya zhǎo ya zhǎo péng you 找呀找呀找朋友,	Look, look, look for friend,
zhǎo dào yī gè hǎo péng you 找到一个好朋友,	Then I find one in the end,
jìng gè lǐ a wò wò shǒu 敬个礼啊握握手,	Salute and shake our hands,
nǐ shì wǒ de hǎo péng you 你是我的好朋友。	You are now my good friend.

学唱中国歌

三 生词详解 (New words)

1. 找　　（动）　　zhǎo　　　　look for
2. 朋友　（名）　　péngyou　　 friend
3. 呀　　（助）　　ya　　　　　ya (auxiliary)
4. 找到　　　　　 zhǎodào　　 find
5. 一　　（数）　　yī　　　　　one
6. 个　　（量）　　gè　　　　　measure word for friends
7. 好　　（形）　　hǎo　　　　 good
8. 敬礼　　　　　 jìng lǐ　　　salute
9. 啊　　（助）　　a　　　　　 a (auxiliary)
10. 握手　　　　　wò shǒu　　 shake hand
11. 是　　（动）　　shì　　　　be
12. 我　　（代）　　wǒ　　　　 I
13. 的　　（助）　　de　　　　 of (possessive particle)

四 歌曲欣赏 (Music sheet)

找朋友

找呀找呀找朋友，找到一个好朋友，
敬个礼啊握握手，你是我的好朋友。

学唱中国歌

五 读一读 (Read the Following Passage)

儿 歌 Children's Ballad

儿歌是儿童口头传唱的歌谣,符合幼儿的理解能力和心理特点,贴近儿童生活,具有歌词简短、易学易记、语言活泼、结构简单、节奏明快、动作性强的特点。

一些儿歌蕴含着丰富的知识,充满着生活情趣,富于游戏性和表演性。通过学唱儿歌不仅使儿童心情愉快,更能够潜移默化地提高他们的想象力和语言表达能力,有助于养成良好的生活习惯和学习习惯。

儿歌也往往是世界性的,很多国外的儿歌已经翻译成汉语。例如郭瑶编译了法国儿歌《两只老虎》:"两只老虎,两只老虎,跑得快,跑得快,一只没有耳朵,一只没有尾巴,真奇怪,真奇怪!"

Children's ballads are sung and passed on by children. These songs are easy for children to accept intellectually and psychologically. They are often about children's lives. The lyrics of a children's ballad are often short and catchy, often with vivid language, simple structure, light tempo and usually goes together with games or other activities.

Some ballads contain rich knowledge, and are filled with love for life. They are often used in games and performances. Children's ballad can not only make children happy, but can also gradually improve their imagination and linguistic expression, encouraging good life habits and study habits.

Children's ballads can also be international, since many foreign ballads have been introduced to China. For example, Guo Yao wrote words for the Chinese version of the French song

学唱中国歌

"Frère Jacques": "Two tigers, two tigers, run very fast, run very fast. One has no ears. One has no tail. How weird is that! How weird is that!"

六 说一说 (Ask and Answer)

1. 在中国,握手是人们见面打招呼的主要方式,在你的国家呢?
2. 除了这首歌,你还听过其他中国儿歌吗?
3. 在你的国家,有哪些有名的儿歌?
4. 和新朋友见面时,你一般怎么打招呼?

七 做一做 (Tasks)

1. 把《找朋友》这首歌曲翻译成自己的母语并演唱。
2. 举例说明儿歌与流行歌曲有哪些不同?

八 词语链接 (Related Words or Phrases)

1.	你好	nǐ hǎo	hello to you
2.	你们好	nǐmen hǎo	hello to (all of) you
3.	您好	nín hǎo	hello (formal/polite)
4.	大家好	dàjiā hǎo	hello to all
5.	谢谢 (动)	xièxie	thanks
6.	不用谢	búyòngxiè	you are welcome
7.	不客气	búkèqi	not at all
8.	对不起 (动)	duìbuqǐ	sorry
9.	没关系	méi guānxi	it does not matter
10.	再见 (动)	zàijiàn	goodbye

学唱中国歌

3 天 堂

Heaven

一 推荐絮语 (Introduction)

这是一首来自大草原的歌,由蒙古族音乐家腾格尔作词作曲并演唱。内蒙古草原十分辽阔,蒙古族世代居住在那里。这首歌具有草原民歌的共同特点,作者把美丽的草原比作天堂,用发自内心的歌声,唱出对故乡深深的爱恋。

This is a song coming from the grand prairie of Inner Mongolia, written and sung by the Mongolian musician Teng Ge'er. The Inner Mongolian Prairie is massive, taking up about one tenth of the total area of China. This is the land where generations of Mongolian people live. The song compares the beautiful grassland to the heaven, which reflects the singer's deep affection of his homeland.

二 歌词对读 (Chinese and English lyrics)

lán lán de tiān kōng
蓝蓝的天空,   Blue blue sky,

qīng qīng de hú shuǐ　āi yē
青青的湖水,哎耶!   Cyan cyan lake, (ei-ye)

lǜ lǜ de cǎo yuán
绿绿的草原,   Green green prairie,

学唱中国歌

zhè shì wǒ de jiā　　āi yē
这是我的家。哎耶！　　This is my home. (ei-ye)

bēn chí de jùn mǎ
奔驰的骏马，　　　　　Galloping horses,

jié bái de yáng qún　āi yē
洁白的羊群，哎耶！　　Snow white sheep, (ei-ye)

hái yǒu nǐ gū niáng
还有你姑娘，　　　　　And the girl, you,

zhè shì wǒ de jiā　āi yē
这是我的家。哎耶！　　This is my home. (ei-ye)

wǒ ài nǐ　wǒ de jiā
我爱你，我的家，　　　I love you, my home,

wǒ de jiā　wǒ de tiān táng
我的家，我的天堂。　　My home, my heaven.

三 生词详解 (New words)

1. 天堂	（名）	tiāntáng	heaven
2. 蓝	（形）	lán	blue
3. 天空	（名）	tiānkōng	sky
4. 青	（形）	qīng	cyan
5. 湖水	（名）	húshuǐ	lake water
6. 绿	（形）	lǜ	green
7. 草原	（名）	cǎoyuán	prairie
8. 这	（代）	zhè	this
9. 家	（名）	jiā	home
10. 奔驰	（动）	bēnchí	gallop, run fast
11. 骏马	（名）	jùnmǎ	a strong and beautiful horse, a gallant horse

学唱中国歌

12. 洁白	（形）	jiébái	spotlessly white
13. 羊群	（名）	yángqún	a herd of sheep
14. 还	（副）	hái	in addition to
15. 有	（动）	yǒu	there be
16. 姑娘	（名）	gūniang	young girl
17. 爱	（动）	ài	love

四 歌曲欣赏 (Music sheet)

天 堂

蓝蓝的天空，　　青青的湖水，哎—
奔腾的骏马，　　洁白的羊群，哎—
耶—！绿绿的草原，这是我的家。哎耶！
耶—！还有你姑娘，这是我的家。哎耶！

我爱你，我的家，我的家，我的天堂。 WOO

学唱中国歌

五 读一读 (Read the Following Passage)

蒙古包 Mongolian Yurt

在辽阔的内蒙古草原上,点缀着许多白色的帐篷,那就是蒙古包。

蒙古包是蒙古族传统的民居,也称"毡包",是一种用厚羊毛毡制成的圆形、凸顶的房屋,一般高约2.5米,直径3米以上。蒙古包是为适应游牧生活而创造的,具有拆装简易、便于搬运、适于游牧的特点。

现在大部分蒙古族已经过上定居生活,不再居住在蒙古包里了。但蒙古包还在一定地区保留着,它已经成为草原特色旅游的一部分,吸引着国内外的游客。如果大家去草原旅游,千万不要忘了住一住蒙古包。当然除了住蒙古包,还可以在草原上骑马、喝奶茶、吃手抓羊肉、尽情地唱歌跳舞。

In the vast grassland of Inner Mongolia, you can find many white tents, which are called "yurts".

The yurt is the traditional architecture of the Mongolians, which is also called "*zhanbao* (felt tent)". Covered with thick felt and a round pointed roof, a yurt is often built 2.5m high and 3m in diameter. This structure is designed for nomadic life, so it is easy to set up or dismantle and is also very portable.

Nowadays most Mongolians have abandoned their yurts and became permanent dwellers. One can still see yurts in some areas, which have become tourist attractions for travelers who want to see life on the grassland. If you are visiting the grassland, remember to spend your night in a yurt. Of course, there are also other interesting

学唱中国歌

things for you to experience there, like horseback-riding, milk tea, eating lamb with your bare hands, singing and dancing, etc.

六 说一说 (Ask and Answer)

1. 为什么作者把自己的故乡比作"天堂"？
2. 你到过草原吗？住过蒙古包吗？
3. 中国是一个多民族国家，你的国家呢？你知道中国有多少个民族吗？

七 做一做 (Tasks)

1. 你知道蒙古族的传统乐器马头琴吗？请查找相关图片和资料。
2. 介绍一下你的家乡。

八 词语链接 (Related Words or Phrases)

1. 红色	（名）	hóngsè	red
2. 黄色	（名）	huángsè	yellow
3. 白色	（名）	báisè	white
4. 黑色	（名）	hēisè	black
5. 灰色	（名）	huīsè	grey
6. 紫色	（名）	zǐsè	purple
7. 粉红色	（名）	fěnhóngsè	pink
8. 棕色	（名）	zōngsè	brown
9. 金色	（名）	jīnsè	golden
10. 银色	（名）	yínsè	silver

学唱中国歌

4 掀起了你的盖头来
Lift Your Veil

一 推荐絮语 (Introduction)

中国共有56个民族,维吾尔族是其中之一。"维吾尔"是汉语译音,它的意思是"团结"或"联合"的意思。维吾尔族是一个能歌善舞的民族,主要居住在新疆维吾尔自治区,那里流传着很多动人的民歌。《掀起你的盖头来》这首歌由被誉为"西部歌王"的王洛宾搜集整理。王洛宾曾说过:"我听了一百首唱姑娘的民歌,我把最优美的一首唱给你,你说怎么能不美?"

There are 56 distinct ethnic groups in China, and Uyghur is one of them. "Weiwu'er" is its Mandarin translation, which means "unite". The Uyghurs, who live mainly in Xinjiang Uyghur Aotonomous Region, are good at singing and dancing. Many appealing folk songs are widespread there. "Lift Your Veil" was a folk song collected by Wang Luobin, who was known as the "king of western folk songs". He once said, "I have heard one hundred songs about young girls, and I sing the finest to you. How can it be not beautiful?"

二 歌词对读 (Chinese and English lyrics)

xiān qǐ le nǐ de gài tou lái
掀起了你的盖头来,　　　　Lift your veil,

学唱中国歌

ràng wǒ lái kàn kàn nǐ de méi
让我来看看你的眉。

nǐ de méi máo xì yòu cháng ya
你的眉毛细又长呀，

hǎo xiàng nà shù shāo de wān yuè liang
好像那树梢的弯月亮。

xiān qǐ le nǐ de gài tou lái
掀起了你的盖头来，

ràng wǒ lái kàn kàn nǐ de yǎn
让我来看看你的眼。

nǐ de yǎn jing míng yòu liàng ya
你的眼睛 明又亮呀，

hǎo xiàng nà qiū bō yī bān yàng
好像那秋波一般样。

xiān qǐ le nǐ de gài tou lái
掀起了你的盖头来，

ràng wǒ lái kàn kàn nǐ de liǎn
让我来看看你的脸。

nǐ de liǎn ér hóng yòu yuán ya
你的脸儿红又圆呀，

hǎo xiàng nà píng guǒ dào qiū tiān
好像那苹果到秋天。

xiān qǐ le nǐ de gài tou lái
掀起了你的盖头来，

ràng wǒ lái kàn kàn nǐ de zuǐ
让我来看看你的嘴。

nǐ de zuǐ ér hóng yòu xiǎo ya
你的嘴儿红又小呀，

hǎo xiàng nà wǔ yuè de hóng yīng táo
好像那五月的红樱桃。

Let me see your brows.

Your brows are so fine and long,

Just like the crescent moon hanging on the end of the tree branches.

Lift your veil,

Let me see your eyes.

Your eyes are so bright and shining,

Just like lake in the fall.

Lift your veil,

Let me see your face.

Your face is red and round,

Like an apple that's ripe.

Lift your veil,

Let me see your mouth.

Your lips are so red and delicate,

Just like the red cherry in May.

学唱中国歌

三 生词详解 (New words)

1.	掀	（动）	xiān	lift
2.	起(来)	（动）	qǐ(lái)	move upward
3.	盖头	（名）	gàitou	bride's veil
4.	让	（介）	ràng	let
5.	眉	（名）	méi	eyebrows
6.	细	（形）	xì	thin, fine
7.	又	（副）	yòu	and
8.	长	（形）	cháng	long
9.	好像	（动）	hǎoxiàng	like, just like
10.	那	（代）	nà	that
11.	树梢	（名）	shùshāo	tip of a tree
12.	弯	（形）	wān	curved
13.	月亮	（名）	yuèliang	moon
14.	眼	（名）	yǎn	eye
15.	明亮	（形）	míngliàng	bright
16.	秋波	（名）	qiūbō	autumn water (used to describe eyes of a girl)
17.	一般样		yībānyàn	the same
18.	脸	（名）	liǎn	face
19.	圆	（形）	yuán	round
20.	苹果	（名）	píngguǒ	apple
21.	秋天	（名）	qiūtiān	autumn
22.	嘴	（名）	zuǐ	mouth
23.	樱桃	（名）	yīngtáo	cherry

学唱中国歌

四 歌曲欣赏 (Music sheet)

掀起了你的盖头来

五 读一读 (Read the Following Passage)

红盖头 Red Bridal Veil

在中国传统文化中，红色表示喜庆吉祥，具有驱邪避凶的作用，因此在婚礼上人们特别喜欢用红色来装饰。而白色是丧服的颜色，婚礼时穿白衣服是绝对不行的。

古时候，在举行婚礼时，都会在新娘头上蒙一块红布或红绸，这块红布或红绸就被称为红盖头。红盖头要在入洞房后由新郎揭开。在古代，由于新郎和新娘结婚前很少有机会见面或者根本没见过面，掀起红盖头的时候，也就是新郎和新娘第一次正式

学唱中国歌

见面，新郎也第一次有机会好好看看自己的新娘。

在现代中国，很多年轻女孩受西方婚俗的影响，都喜欢白色的婚纱。穿传统中式礼服的人也越来越少，更没有人蒙红盖头了。

In traditional Chinese culture, the color red symbolizes celebration and fortune. It is believed that using red in a wedding helps chase away devils and avoids bad luck. The color white, on the other hand, is used in funerals, and therefore could never be seen in a wedding ceremony.

In ancient times, when a wedding ceremony begins, the bride's head is covered by a piece of red cloth or red silk, which is referred to as the "red bridal veil" and the veil is lifted by the groom when he enters the bedroom. In the past, the bride and groom seldom or never meet until the wedding, so when the veil is lifted, the bride and groom meet officially. The groom gets a chance to take a good look at his bride for the first time.

In modern China, many girls, influenced by western wedding culture, prefer white gowns for their wedding. Less and less people wear traditional Chinese costumes in wedding ceremonies, and even fewer wear a red veil.

六 说一说 (Ask and Answer)

1. 歌曲中用哪些事物来比喻姑娘的眉、眼、脸、嘴？
2. 在中国古代，举行婚礼时新娘为什么在头上盖一块红布？
3. 在中国，人们对婚礼服装的颜色有没有偏好？在你的国家呢？

学唱中国歌

七 做一做 (Tasks)

1. 你知道中国人结婚时穿的传统礼服是什么样的吗？请查找相关图片和资料。
2. 介绍一下你的国家婚礼的礼服等。

八 词语链接 (Related Words or Phrases)

1. 头发	（名）	tóufa	hair
2. 眼睛	（名）	yǎnjing	eye
3. 耳朵	（名）	ěrduo	ear
4. 鼻子	（名）	bízi	nose
5. 舌头	（名）	shétou	tongue
6. 嘴唇	（名）	zuǐchún	lip
7. 牙齿	（名）	yáchǐ	tooth
8. 前额	（名）	qián'é	forehead
9. 脸颊	（名）	liǎnjiá	cheek
10. 脖子	（名）	bózi	neck

学唱中国歌

5 达坂城的姑娘
The Girl from Dabancheng

一 推荐絮语 (Introduction)

《达坂城的姑娘》是王洛宾搜集改编的最优美的新疆民歌之一。1939年,王洛宾在兰州初次听到一个维吾尔族司机唱吐鲁番民歌《达坂城》,立刻被吸引住了。他边听边记,然后又对歌曲进行了改编,重新配上了歌词,就成了今天的《达坂城的姑娘》(也叫《马车夫之恋》)。这首歌曲调轻快、歌词活泼,很快传遍全国,达坂城和达坂城的姑娘也因此名扬天下。

The Girl from Dabancheng is one of the most beautiful Xinjiang folk songs collected and composed by Wang Luobin. In 1939 in the city of Lanzhou, Wang heard a Uyghur driver sing the Tulufan folk song *Dabancheng*. He was immediately interested and recorded the music as he listened. After making some adjustments to the music, he gave new lyrics to the melody, which is the song we hear today: *The Girl from Dabancheng* (also called *Romance of the Coachman*). With its delightful tunes and lively lyrics, the song soon got popular nationwide, and the little town of Dabancheng and its girls became famous.

学唱中国歌

二 歌词对读 (Chinese and English lyrics)

dá bǎn chéng de shí lù yìng yòu píng ya
达坂城的石路硬又平呀，
The stone road in Dabancheng is flat and hard,

xī guā dà yòu tián ya
西瓜大又甜呀。
The watermelon there is sweet and large.

nà lǐ de gū niang biàn zǐ cháng ya
那里的姑娘辫子长呀，
The girls there have long hair,

liǎng zhī yǎn jing zhēn piào liang
两只眼睛真漂亮。
All of whom have beautiful eyes.

rú guǒ nǐ yào jià rén
如果你要嫁人，
If you are going to marry,

bú yào jià gěi bié ren
不要嫁给别人，
Don't marry other men,

yí dìng yào jià gěi wǒ
一定要嫁给我。
Be sure to marry me.

dài zhe nǐ de jià zhuang
带着你的嫁妆，
Bring your dowries,

lǐng zhe nǐ de mèi mei
领着你的妹妹，
Take your sister,

gǎn zhe nà mǎ chē lái
赶着那马车来。
Arrive in a horse-drawn cart.

三 生词详解 (New words)

1. 达坂城　　（专名）　　Dábǎn Chéng　　a town's name
2. 石路　　　（名）　　　shílù　　　　　stone road
3. 硬　　　　（形）　　　yìng　　　　　hard
4. 平　　　　（形）　　　píng　　　　　flat

学唱中国歌

5.	西瓜	（名）	xīguā	watermelon
6.	大	（形）	dà	big, large
7.	甜	（形）	tián	sweet
8.	那里	（名）	nàlǐ	there
9.	辫子	（名）	biànzi	plait
10.	只	（量）	zhī	measure word for eyes
11.	漂亮	（形）	piàoliang	pretty
12.	如果	（连）	rúguǒ	if
13.	要	（动）	yào	will
14.	嫁	（动）	jià	marry
15.	给	（介、动）	gěi	to; give
16.	别人	（代）	biéren	others
17.	一定	（副）	yīdìng	be sure to, must
18.	带	（动）	dài	bring
19.	着	（助）	zhe	particle indicating action in progress
20.	嫁妆	（名）	jiàzhuang	dowry
21.	领	（动）	lǐng	take, bring, lead
22.	妹妹	（名）	mèimei	sister
23.	马车	（名）	mǎchē	horse-drown cart
24.	来	（动）	lái	come

学唱中国歌

四 歌曲欣赏 (Music sheet)

达坂城的姑娘

达坂城的石路硬又平呀，西瓜大又甜呀。

那里的姑娘辫子长呀，两只眼睛真漂亮。

如果你要嫁人，不要嫁给别人，一定要嫁给我。

带着你的嫁妆，领着你的妹妹，赶着那马车来。

五 读一读 (Read the Following Passage)

维吾尔族的木卡姆 Uyghur Muqam

木卡姆是一种集歌、舞、乐于一体的大型综合艺术形式，是流传于新疆维吾尔族各聚居区的"十二木卡姆"、"刀郎木卡姆"、"吐鲁番木卡姆"和"哈密木卡姆"等的总称，在整个新疆地区广为流传。

木卡姆的唱词包括哲人箴言、先知告诫、乡村俚语、民间故事等，集文学、历史、音乐、舞蹈和生活习俗与一体，是维吾尔族人民生活智慧的体现。它的音乐形态丰富，有多种音律，繁复的

学唱中国歌

调式、节拍、节奏和组合形式多样的伴奏乐器，显示出鲜明的民族特色和强烈的感染力，素有"东方音乐明珠"的美称。2005年入选联合国教科文组织"人类口头和非物质遗产代表作"。

Muqam, a complex suite combining singing, dancing and instrument-playing, is a generic name used for music forms like "On Ikki Muqam", "Dolan Muqam", "Turfan Muqam", "Kumul Muqam", etc., which is popular in the area of Xinjiang.

The lyrics of muqam include philosophers' maxims, prophets' warnings, slang and folk tales. It embodies literature, history, music, dancing and lifestyle, and is the collective representation of Uyghur people's wisdom in life. It consists of complex music forms of melodies, tones, tempos, rhythmic patterns and combinations of instruments, with distinctive Uyghur characteristics and great appeal. It is called "the pearl of Oriental music". In November 2005 the Art of Uyghur Muqam was named a Masterpiece of the Oral and Intangible Heritage of Humanity by UNESCO.

六 说一说 (Ask and Answer)

1. 什么是嫁妆？在你的国家，结婚时女方要准备什么嫁妆？
2. 在你的国家，结婚时男方一般要准备什么？
3. 在你的国家，有没有一些特殊的婚俗？
4. 你觉得什么样的发型、脸型、眉、眼最漂亮？

学唱中国歌

七 做一做 (Tasks)

1. 介绍一下维吾尔族的"木卡姆"。
2. 歌曲中唱道:"你要是嫁人,不要嫁给别人,一定要嫁给我,带着你的嫁妆,带着你的妹妹,赶着那马车来。"你知道为什么要"带着你的妹妹"吗?请根据伊斯兰教的婚姻习俗查找资料并思考。

八 词语链接 (Related Words or Phrases)

1.	梨	(名)	lí	pear
2.	橘子	(名)	júzi	orange
3.	香蕉	(名)	xiāngjiāo	banana
4.	菠萝	(名)	bōluó	pineapple
5.	葡萄	(名)	pútao	grape
6.	草莓	(名)	cǎoméi	strawberry
7.	桃子	(名)	táozi	peach
8.	柠檬	(名)	níngméng	lemon
9.	石榴	(名)	shíliu	pomegranate
10.	柿子	(名)	shìzi	persimmon

学唱中国歌

6 月儿弯弯照九州

Crescent Moon over China

一 推荐絮语 (Introduction)

这是一首流传在江苏一带的民歌，据说出自南宋建炎年间（1127—1130），已经传唱了几百年。这首歌以对话的形式，讲述了民间离乱之苦，真实地记录了百姓的心声。

"Crescent Moon over China" is a Jiangsu folk song, which is believed to have originated from as early as Jianyan Period (1127—1130), Nan Song dynasty. Its lyrics are composed of dialogue, telling about people's bitter life in an unstable society, and provides a genuine record of common people's thoughts.

二 歌词对读 (Chinese and English lyrics)

yuè ér wān wān zhào jiǔ zhōu
月儿弯弯照九州，
Crescent moon is shining over China,

jǐ jiā huān lè jǐ jiā chóu
几家欢乐几家愁。
How many families are happy? How many are in agony?

jǐ jiā gāo lóu yǐn měi jiǔ
几家高楼饮美酒，
How many families are enjoying fine wine in grand buildings?

jǐ jiā liú làng zài wài tou
几家流浪在外头。
How many people are drifting, far away from home?

学唱中国歌

yuè ér wān wān zhào jiǔ zhōu
月儿弯弯照九州，

jǐ jiā huān lè jǐ jiā chóu
几家欢乐几家愁。

jǐ jiā fū qī tuán yuán jù
几家夫妻团圆聚，

jǐ jiā liú luò zài jiē tóu
几家流落在街头。

Crescent moon is shining over China,

How many families are happy? How many are in agony?

How many couples are celebrating their reunion?

How many are wandering on the streets and couldn't go home?

三 生词详解 (New words)

1.	月儿	（名）	yuè'ér	moon
2.	照	（动）	zhào	light, shine
3.	九州	（专名）	Jiǔzhōu	China mainland
4.	几	（数）	jǐ	how many
5.	家	（量、名）	jiā	family
6.	欢乐	（形）	huānlè	joyful, happy
7.	愁	（动、名）	chóu	worry, sad
8.	高楼	（名）	gāolóu	tall building
9.	饮	（动）	yǐn	drink
10.	美酒	（名）	měijiǔ	fine wine
11.	流浪	（动）	liúlàng	lead a vagrant life
12.	在	（介、动）	zài	at
13.	外头	（名）	wàitou	outside, away from home
14.	夫妻	（名）	fūqī	husband and wife, couple

学唱中国歌

15.	团圆	（动、形）	tuányuán	family get together, reunion
16.	聚	（动）	jù	get together
17.	流落	（动）	liúluò	wander
18.	街头	（名）	jiētóu	street, street corner

四 歌曲欣赏 (Music sheet)

月儿弯弯照九州

学唱中国歌

五 读一读 (Read the Following Passage)

中秋节和月饼 Mid-Autumn Day and Mooncake

中秋节在农历的八月十五日,它是中国仅次于春节的第二大传统节日,全国放假一天。农历的七、八、九三个月为秋季,八月十五日正好是秋季的中间,"中秋"因此得名。秋季是收获的季节,人们尽情享受丰收的喜悦。中国自古就有在中秋节时全家团圆、宴饮赏月的习俗,因此中秋节也被称为"团圆节"。

月饼是中国人中秋佳节必食之品。如果在中国看到满街满铺的月饼,那就意味着中秋节即将来临了。月饼是仿照圆月的形状制成的糕点,里面有馅,又香又甜,象征着团圆、吉祥。月饼在中国的不同地方逐渐形成了各自不同的风味,不但形状、大小各不相同,馅儿和味道更是花样各异:有甜有咸,有大有小,大的一个就有几斤重,小的几个才一两重。南方的月饼馅儿多用鸭蛋黄、咸肉、火腿,北方则多用小枣、豆沙。现在,月饼已经不再是中秋节才有的食品,一年四季都可买到。

The Mid-Autumn Day falls on the 15th day of the 8th lunar month of the Chinese calendar. It is the second largest national traditional festival in China, and a legal holiday, too. By the lunar calendar, autumn lasts from the 7th to the 9th month, and that day comes right in the middle of the season. Autumn is the season of the harvest, when people are enjoying the happiness of abundance. From ancient times, Chinese families developed the custom of

学唱中国歌

getting together and admiring the full moon, and that is why the Mid-autumn Day is also called "the day of togetherness".

Mooncakes are eaten by almost every Chinese on that day. If you see mooncakes being sold in every store on the street, you know that Mid-Autumn Day is drawing near. Mooncake, a pastry with thick fillings, is made in the shape of a full moon. It is delicious and sweet, and symbolizes togetherness and good luck. Mooncakes in different parts of China have developed various local flavors (sweet or salty), and they also differ in shape and size (from several kilos to tens of grams each). Most mooncakes in southern China have duck egg yolk, salty meat and bacon in the fillings, while in the north people stuff date and bean paste inside. Nowadays, mooncake is no longer a special food only served in that particular period of the year, and one can get it almost all year round.

六 说一说 (Ask and Answer)

1. "几家欢乐几家愁"是什么意思？
2. 在你的国家,有没有这种讲述离别之苦或思念亲人的歌？
3. 你吃过月饼吗？月饼是什么样的？
4. 为什么月饼是中国人中秋节必吃的食品？

七 做一做 (Tasks)

1. 中国人过传统节日时常有一些必吃的食品,你知道中国人过春节(农历一月一日)、元宵节(农历一月十五日)和端午节(农历五月五日)时分别要吃什么吗？

学唱中国歌

2. 在中国留学,你思念家里的亲人吗?试着用中文唱这首歌并翻译成你的母语。

八 词语链接 (Related Words or Phrases)

1.	佳节	(名)	jiājié	festival
2.	思念	(动)	sīniàn	miss
3.	亲人	(名)	qīnrén	relative
4.	爱人	(名)	àirén	lover
5.	平安	(形)	píng'ān	safe
6.	归来	(动)	guīlái	return
7.	中秋节	(专名)	Zhōngqiūjié	Mid-Autumn Day
8.	月饼	(名)	yuèbing	moon cake
9.	农历	(名)	nónglì	lunar calendar
10.	吉祥	(形)	jíxiáng	auspicious

学唱中国歌

7 茉莉花
Jasmine

一 推荐絮语 (Introduction)

《茉莉花》是人们喜听爱唱的一首民歌小调,流传于全国。早在18世纪就被翻译介绍到海外,是最早流传到海外的中国歌曲。各地的《茉莉花》有不同的曲调,各具特点,但歌词基本相同,都以反映男女纯真的感情为内容。本曲是何仿在江苏民歌《鲜花调》的基础上整理的。

Jasmine is among the most popular Chinese folk songs, and was once given the title of "the second national anthem". From as early as the 18th century, it had been introduced to countries outside China. The song has different versions sung by people in different areas of China, though the lyrics are basically the same. It is a song depicting the innocent hearts of young boys and girls. The version introduced here is based on the Jiangsu folk song *A Tune of Fresh Flowers* (Xianhua Diao) collected by the musician He Fang.

二 歌词对读 (Chinese and English lyrics)

hǎo yī duǒ měi lì de mò lì huā
好一朵美丽的茉莉花,　　What a beautiful jasmine flower,
hǎo yī duǒ měi lì de mò lì huā
好一朵美丽的茉莉花,　　What a beautiful jasmine flower,

学唱中国歌

fēn fāng měi lì mǎn zhī yā
芬芳美丽满枝桠， With sweet smell and pretty flowers blooming all over branches,

yòu xiāng yòu bái rén rén kuā
又香又白人人夸。 Fragrant and white that wins everyone's praises.

ràng wǒ lái jiāng nǐ zhāi xià
让我来将你摘下， Let me pick you,

sòng gěi bié rén jiā
送给别人家。 And give you to someone.

mò lì huā ya mò lì huā
茉莉花呀茉莉花！ Jasmine flower, oh, jasmine flower!

三 生词详解 (New words)

1.	朵	（量）	duǒ	measure word for flower
2.	茉莉花	（名）	mòlìhuā	jasmine
3.	芬芳	（形）	fēnfāng	with fragrant and sweet smell
4.	满	（形）	mǎn	full
5.	枝桠	（名）	zhīyā	branch
6.	香	（名）	xiāng	fragrance
7.	夸	（动）	kuā	praise
8.	将	（介）	jiāng	a marker for object
9.	摘	（动）	zhāi	pick, pluck

学唱中国歌

四 歌曲欣赏 (Music sheet)

茉莉花

好一朵美丽的茉莉花,好一朵美丽的茉莉花,芬芳美丽满枝桠,又香又白人人夸。让我来将你摘下,送给别人家。茉莉花呀茉莉花!

学唱中国歌

五 读一读 (Read the Following Passage)

牡 丹 Peony

牡丹有"花王"、"国色天香"的美称,是中国最负盛名的花卉之一。它雍容华贵,端庄富丽,色香俱全,观赏价值极高,一直被看作是吉祥昌盛的象征,所以人们常称之为"富贵花"。

牡丹在中国已有一千五百多年的栽培史,一直受到大家的喜爱。唐代大诗人白居易的诗中就写到"花开花落二十日,一城之人皆若狂"。说明早在唐朝时,牡丹花季就成了首都长安(现在西安)的狂欢节。

河南洛阳、山东菏泽、四川彭县等地都盛产牡丹,其中以洛阳最为有名。牡丹花不仅是洛阳的市花,更是这座城市的"名片",提到牡丹花,人们便想到洛阳。洛阳自1983年起每年举办牡丹花会,至今已经举办了26届,每年都吸引着数千万的游客前往观赏、游览。

Peony, one of the most famous flowers of China, is also called "the king of flowers" or "the color of kingdom, the scent of heaven". Coming in various colors and smells and symbolizing fortune and prosperity, it is also referred to as "the flower of riches and honor".

Peony has been cultivated in China from as early as 1,500 years ago and has always been admired by Chinese people. Bai Juyi, the famous poet in Tang Dynasty, once wrote: "During the twenty days peonies bloom, the whole city goes crazy for it", which shows that from as early as the Tang Dynasty, peony-blooming season was

学唱中国歌

celebrated as a festival in the capital city of Chang'an (now Xi'an).

Luoyang in Henan province, Heze in Shandong province, and Pengxian in Sichuan province are all cultivation centers of peony, among which Luoyang is the most well-known. Peony is the city flower and city name card of Luoyang, i.e. whenever people think of peony, inevitably, they will think of the city. Since 1983, Luoyang holds a peony flower show each year. Every year, in the past 26 years, thousands of visitors go to the show.

六 说一说 (Ask and Answer)

1. 在满园花中作者为什么最喜欢茉莉花？你喜欢什么花？
2. 为什么说牡丹是洛阳市的"名片"？
3. 你的国家有没有国花？你所在的城市有没有市花？

七 做一做 (Tasks)

1. 在中国，一些花具有文化象征意义，比如，荷花象征着纯洁。你知道下面这些植物各有什么象征意义吗？
    兰花
    玫瑰花
    菊花
    梅花
    松树
    竹子
2. 介绍一下你的国家的国花并查找相关资料和图片。

学唱中国歌

八 词语链接 (Related Words or Phrases)

1. 玫瑰	（名）	méigui	rose
2. 牡丹	（名）	mǔdan	peony
3. 梅花	（名）	méihuā	plum blossom
4. 月季	（名）	yuèjì	China rose
5. 荷花	（名）	héhuā	lotus
6. 菊花	（名）	júhuā	chrysanthemum
7. 百合花	（名）	bǎihéhuā	lily
8. 兰花	（名）	lánhuā	orchid
9. 水仙	（名）	shuǐxiān	narcissus
10. 郁金香	（名）	yùjīnxiāng	tulip

学唱中国歌

8 爱情鸟
Love Bird

一 推荐絮语 (Introduction)

爱情鸟是一种什么鸟啊？其实它并不是真的鸟，作者只是用它来比喻爱情。这个比喻非常新颖独特，因此《爱情鸟》（张海宁作词，张全复作曲）这首歌一下子就抓住了很多听众的心。歌曲抒发了对爱情的追求与向往，尽管"爱情鸟"已经飞走了，歌曲却并没有以痛苦悲伤的形式出现，而是显得非常乐观开朗，相信有一天"爱情鸟"一定会来到。

A love bird is not a special kind of bird; the writer of the song only used it metaphorically for love, which shows initiative. The song (lyrics by Zhang Haining, music by Zhang Quanfu) soon caught many listeners' hearts. It sings about people's pursuit of and longing for love, even when it has already "flown" away. The song does not show any suffering for the lost love, but an optimistic sanguinity prevails, believing that one day the "love bird" will surely come.

二 歌词对读 (Chinese and English lyrics)

shù shàng tíng zhe yī zhī yī zhī shén me niǎo
树上停着一只一只什么鸟？ What kind of a bird is sitting in the tree?

学唱中国歌

hū hū hū ràng wǒ jué de xīn zài tiào
呼呼呼,让我觉得心在跳。 Hoo hoo hoo, it makes me feel my heartbeat.

wǒ kàn bú jiàn tā
我看不见她, I cannot see her,

dàn què tīng de dào
但却听得到, But I can hear her,

hū hū hū zhè zhī ài qíng niǎo
呼呼呼,这只爱情鸟, Hoo hoo hoo, this is the love bird,

tā zài xiàng wǒ huān jiào
她在向我欢叫。 She is singing cheerfully to me,

shù shàng tíng zhe yī zhī yī zhī shén me niǎo
树上停着一只一只什么鸟? What kind of a bird is sitting in the tree?

hū hū hū rú jīn biàn de jìng qiāoqiāo
呼呼呼,如今变得静悄悄, Hoo hoo hoo, It becomes so quiet now,

yīn wèi wǒ ài de rén yǐ jīng bú jiàn le
因为我爱的人已经不见了, Because my loved one is gone now,

hū hū hū zhè zhī ài qíng niǎo
呼呼呼,这只爱情鸟, Hoo hoo hoo, this is the love bird,

hé shí cái huì lái dào
何时才会来到? When will it finally come to me?

wǒ ài de rén yǐ jīng fēi zǒu le
我爱的人已经飞走了, My loved one has flown away,

ài wǒ de rén tā hái méi yǒu lái dào
爱我的人她还没有来到。 The one who loves me has not yet come.

zhè zhī ài qíngniǎo yǐ jīng fēi zǒu le
这只爱情鸟已经飞走了, This love bird is gone now,

wǒ de ài qíngniǎo tā hái méi lái dào
我的爱情鸟她还没来到。 My love bird is here not yet.

学唱中国歌

三 生词详解 (New words)

1. 爱情　　（名）　àiqíng　　　　love
2. 鸟　　　（名）　niǎo　　　　　bird
3. 树　　　（名）　shù　　　　　 tree
4. 停　　　（动）　tíng　　　　　stop
5. 什么　　（代）　shénme　　　　what
6. 觉得　　（动）　juéde　　　　 feel, suppose, think
7. 心　　　（名）　xīn　　　　　 heart
8. 跳　　　（动）　tiào　　　　　beat, jump
9. 但　　　（连）　dàn　　　　　 but
10. 却　　（副）　què　　　　　 yet
11. 向　　（介、动）xiàng　　　　toward, to
12. 欢叫　（动）　huānjiào　　　 to sing cheerfully
13. 如今　（名）　rújīn　　　　　now
14. 变　　（动）　biàn　　　　　 become
15. 静悄悄（形）　jìngqiāoqiāo　 quiet, silent
16. 因为　（连）　yīnwèi　　　　 because
17. 已经　（副）　yǐjīng　　　　 already
18. 何时　（名）　héshí　　　　　when
19. 才　　（副）　cái　　　　　　just, not until
20. 会　　（动）　huì　　　　　　will

学唱中国歌

四 歌曲欣赏 (Music sheet)

爱情鸟

学唱中国歌

五 读一读 (Read the Following Passage)

鸳 鸯 Mandarin Duck

文化象征寓意的运用是中国传统文化的一大特色，生活中的一些动物、植物或物品都具有一定的文化象征意义，如龙象征着皇帝和皇权，石榴象征着多子多福，花瓶象征着平平安安等。

鸳鸯本是一种常见的水鸟，但由于雌雄总是成双成对出现，形影不离，就像恩爱的夫妻一样，所以在中国文化中，它被认为是爱情鸟。

早在唐朝，鸳鸯就成为民间的吉祥物，被看作是对爱情忠贞不渝、夫妻恩爱的象征。在新婚洞房里少不了各种鸳鸯图案，如鸳鸯枕、鸳鸯帐、鸳鸯被。"鸳鸯戏水"是对新人恩爱到老的美好的祝愿；"只羡鸳鸯不羡仙"是人们对爱情的渴望；"鸳鸯衔莲花"常被人们称做"鸳鸯贵子"，比喻夫妇和美，子孙富贵。

In traditional Chinese culture, many animals, plants and objects have symbolic meanings. For example, the dragon symbolizes emperor and imperial authority, the pomegranate symbolizes fertility, and the vase symbolizes security and peace.

A mandarin duck is a common water bird. Because the male and female always appear in pairs and huddle together, like loving couples, in traditional Chinese culture, they are regarded as love birds.

From as early as the Tang Dynasty, mandarin ducks, as a folk mascot, have been regarded as a symbol of fidelity and conjugal affection. In a newly-wedded couple's bedroom, it is easy to find

学唱中国歌

pillows, curtains, and bedclothes featuring mandarin ducks. There are many Chinese proverbs. "Two mandarin ducks playing in water" is a wish for couples to live happily ever after; "to envy the mandarin ducks not the celestials" conveys people's yearning for love; "a mandarin duck with a lotus flower in its beak" or "mandarin duck and a son with noble character" are both metaphors for harmonious couples and wealthy descendants.

六 说一说 (Ask and Answer)

1. 你相信"一见钟情"吗？你所希望的爱情是什么样的？
2. 在你的国家有哪些爱情歌曲？
3. "鸳鸯"为什么被看成是爱情的象征？
4. 在你的国家,恋人之间会互相赠送什么样的礼物？

七 做一做 (Tasks)

1. 你知道下面这些飞禽走兽在汉语中各有什么象征意义吗？
   凤
   喜鹊
   乌鸦
   蝙蝠
   龙
   乌龟
2. 介绍一下你的国家含有象征意义的动物并查找相关资料和图片。

学唱中国歌

八 词语链接 (Related Words or Phrases)

1.	鸳鸯	（名）	yuānyang	mandarin duck
2.	鹦鹉	（名）	yīngwǔ	parrot
3.	喜鹊	（名）	xǐquè	magpie
4.	麻雀	（名）	máquè	sparrow
5.	猫头鹰	（名）	māotóuyīng	owl
6.	老鹰	（名）	lǎoyīng	hawk
7.	孔雀	（名）	kǒngquè	peacock
8.	燕子	（名）	yànzi	swallow
9.	大雁	（名）	dàyàn	wild goose
10.	天鹅	（名）	tiān'é	swan

学唱中国歌

9 糊涂的爱
Muddled Love

一 推荐絮语 (Introduction)

《糊涂的爱》(张和平作词，王小勇作曲)是电视连续剧《过把瘾》的主题歌。这首歌的歌词虽然简单直白，但却耐人寻味。爱情到底是什么？可能没有几个人能说清楚。不过真挚的爱情一定是互相关心、互相谦让、互相包容的，夫妻双方不能斤斤计较，该糊涂的时候千万不要太精明，当然该明白的时候也千万不能犯糊涂。

"*Muddled Love*" (lyrics by Zhang Heping, music by Wang Xiaoyong) is the theme song of the TV series "*Give it a Shot*". Lyrics of this song are simple and frank, and at the same time thought provoking. What is love? Probably nobody could tell. But genuine love means mutual care, giving and tolerance. Couples should not "haggle over every ounce", and sometimes in love, it is wiser to be a fool.

二 歌词对读 (Chinese and English lyrics)

ài yǒu jǐ fēn néng shuō qīng chu
爱有几分能说清楚， How much can you understand about love,

学唱中国歌

<tr>
hái yǒu jǐ fēn shì hú lǐ yòu hú tu
还有几分是糊里又糊涂。
When sometimes knowing love is tough.

qíng yǒu jǐ fēn shì wēn cún
情有几分是温存，
Part of the emotion is tender,

hái yǒu jǐ fēn shì sè sè de suān chǔ
还有几分是涩涩的酸楚。
While the other part is bitter.

wàng bú diào de yī mù yī mù
忘不掉的一幕一幕，
Those scenes between us are hard to forget,

què liú bú zhù wǎng rì de wēn dù
却留不住往日的温度。
The passion we used to have escapes the grip.

yì niàn zhōng de rè rè hū hū
意念中的热热乎乎，
The warm feeling I still remember,

shì zhēn shì jiǎ shì tián hái shi kǔ
是真是假是甜还是苦。
But it's hard to tell whether it is real or fake, sweet or bitter.

zhè jiù shì ài shuō yě shuō bu qīng chu
这就是爱，说也说不清楚。
This is love, which is hard to tell.

zhè jiù shì ài hú li yòu hú tu
这就是爱，糊里又糊涂。
This is love, which is muddled.

zhè jiù shì ài tā wàng jì le rén jiān
这就是爱，他忘记了人间
de fán nǎo
的烦恼。
This is love, in which you forget all your cares.

zhè jiù shì ài néng bǎo chí zhe hú tu
这就是爱，能保持着糊涂
de wēn dù
的温度。
This is love, sometimes you have to feel like a fool.

wàng bú diào de yī mù yī mù
忘不掉的一幕一幕，
Those scenes between us are hard to forget,

学唱中国歌

却留不住往日的温度。	The passion we used to have escapes the grip.
意念中的热热乎乎，	The warm feeling I still remember,
是真是假是甜还是苦？	But it's hard to tell whether it is real or fake, sweet or bitter?
这就是爱，说也说不清楚。	This is love, which is hard to tell.
这就是爱，糊里又糊涂。	This is love, which is muddled.
这就是爱，能托起人间的脆弱。	This is love, in which those who are fragile get supported.
这就是爱，他再累也不觉得苦。	This is love, in which one feels happy even when tired.
这就是爱，说也说不清楚。	This is love, which is hard to tell.
这就是爱，糊里又糊涂。	This is love, which is muddled.
这就是爱，他忘记了人间的烦恼。	This is love, in which you forget all your cares.

三 生词详解 (New words)

1. 糊涂　　　（形、动）　　　hútu　　stupid, muddled

学唱中国歌

2.	几分		jǐ fēn	a bit, somewhat
3.	糊里糊涂	（形）	húlihútu	muddle-headed
4.	温存	（形）	wēncún	gentle, tender
5.	涩	（形）	sè	(taste) astringent
6.	酸楚	（名）	suānchǔ	feeling bitter and miserable at heart
7.	忘掉	（动）	wàngdiào	forget
8.	幕	（量、名）	mù	scene
9.	往日	（名）	wǎngrì	past days
10.	温度	（名）	wēndù	temperature
11.	意念	（名）	yìniàn	idea, thought
12.	热乎	（形）	rèhu	warm
13.	人间	（名）	rénjiān	man's world
14.	烦恼	（名）	fánnǎo	trouble, care
15.	托起	（动）	tuōqǐ	to support from under
16.	脆弱	（形）	cuìruò	vulnerable, fragile

四 歌曲欣赏 (Music sheet)

糊涂的爱

学唱中国歌

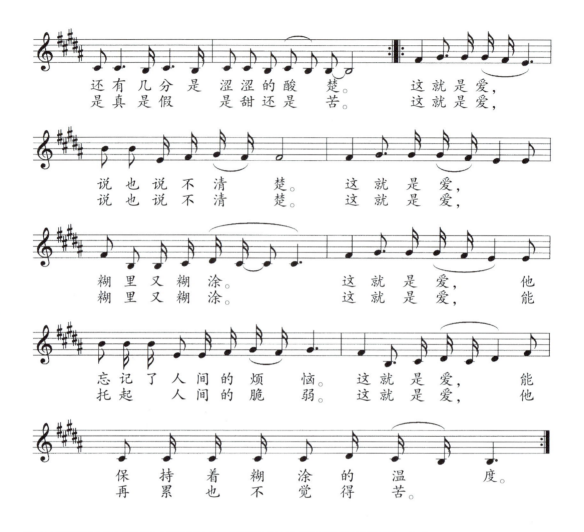

五 读一读 (Read the Following Passage)

难得糊涂 Nan De Hu Tu

郑板桥是清代著名书画家,曾题写过很多匾额,其中最脍炙人口的是"难得糊涂"和"吃亏是福"这两块。在很多中国人家里,都悬挂着他的草书"难得糊涂"。"糊涂"本来是指不明白、不清楚的意思,可为什么却被很多中国人奉为至理名言呢?

要想理解"难得糊涂"的意思,还得参考郑板桥在"难得糊涂"下面加的注解:"聪明难,糊涂难,由聪明而转入糊涂更难,放

学唱中国歌

一着,退一步,当下心安,非图后来福报也。"可见这里的"糊涂"不是真糊涂,而是装糊涂,明明  是非常清楚明白,却装作不明不白,即"由聪明而转入糊涂"。

"难得糊涂"体现了郑板桥的处世哲学:有些事情,不必或不能过于认真,能在不必认真的时候做到糊涂,那才是聪明。

Zheng Banqiao, the famous calligraphist and painter of Qing Dynasty, has many calligraphy works left behind, the most popular of which are "Nan de hu tu (It is difficult to be muddle-headed)" and "Chi kui shi fu (It is good luck being taken advantage of)". Copies of "Nan de hu tu" can often be seen hanging on the walls in Chinese people's homes. "Hu tu" means "do not understand or being unclear about". Why this saying is considered a maxim of wisdom in China?

In order to understand what Zheng really meant, we have to read the explanation he wrote under "Nan de hu tu", "It is difficult to be smart, while it is more difficult to be muddle-headed, and even more difficult is turning from being smart to being muddle-headed. One does not let go or take a step back with the intent of good luck in the future; one does that simply for peace and harmony of heart at the moment." Therefore we know "being muddle-headed" does not mean "being dumb", but means "pretending to be muddled and let go". It is real wisdom if you can "turn from being smart to being muddled".

学唱中国歌

"Nan de hu tu" reflects Zheng's philosophy of dealing with matters in the society: one should not focus too much on trivial things, and being "too smart" is not as desirable as being a little "muddle-headed".

六 说一说 (Ask and Answer)

1. 你认为爱是"糊涂"的吗?
2. 歌曲中"涩涩的酸楚"是指什么?
3. 你同意"只要有爱,再累也不觉得苦"这种观点吗?
4. 你觉得恋人或夫妻之间应该怎样相处?

七 做一做 (Tasks)

1. "难得糊涂"是什么意思?你愿意做个"糊涂"的人吗?
2. 你知道中国人说的"吃亏是福"是什么意思吗?介绍一下你的国家的婚恋观?

八 词语链接 (Related Words or Phrases)

1. 真挚	(形)	zhēnzhì	sincere
2. 关心	(动)	guānxīn	care
3. 谦让	(动)	qiānràng	to modestly decline
4. 包容	(动)	bāoróng	tolerant
5. 斤斤计较		jīnjīn jìjiào	to haggle over every ounce, to be particular about trifle

学唱中国歌

6. 难得　　　（形）　　nándé　　　　　hard to come by
7. 精明　　　（形）　　jīngmíng　　　　smart
8. 装糊涂　　　　　　　zhuāng hútu　　to pretend not to know, to play the fool
9. 至理名言　　　　　　zhìlǐ míngyán　wise saying
10. 处世哲学　　　　　　chǔshì zhéxué　philosophy of life

学唱中国歌

10 弯弯的月亮
The Crescent Moon

一 推荐絮语 (Introduction)

《弯弯的月亮》(李海鹰作词作曲)是一首曲调优美、富有画面感的思乡曲。主人公在弯弯的月亮下回忆遥远的家乡和梦中的女孩。岁月匆匆,在朦胧的月光中,浓浓的乡思和童年的往事悄然浮现在他的脑海中。

The Crescent Moon (lyrics and music by Li Haiying) is a beautiful song with a picturesque and nostalgic tune. Under the crescent moon, the singer is thinking about his hometown far away and the girl of his dreams. Time flies by, and under the hazy moon those old pictures of his home and youth quietly emerge in his mind.

二 歌词对读 (Chinese and English lyrics)

yáo yuǎn de yè kōng
遥远的夜空, — Far away in the night sky,

yǒu yī gè wān wān de yuè liang
有一个弯弯的月亮。 — Hang a hook of crescent.

wān wān de yuè liang xià mian
弯弯的月亮下面, — Beneath that crescent,

shì nà wān wān de xiǎo qiáo
是那弯弯的小桥。 — Stood the arch of a little bridge.

xiǎo qiáo de páng biān
小桥的旁边, — Next to the little bridge,

学唱中国歌

有一条弯弯的小船。   Swayed a pointy boat.

弯弯的小船悠悠，   The pointy boat gently swung,

是那童年的阿娇。   That Little Rose of my childhood.

阿娇摇着船，   Little Rose rowed the boat,

唱着那古老的歌谣。   Singing that ancient lullaby.

歌声随风飘啊，   Her voice scattered into the wind,

飘到我的脸上。   Touching my face.

脸上淌着泪，   My face was awash with tears,

像那条弯弯的河水。   Like that stream of winding river.

弯弯的河水流啊，   The winding river roamed about,

流进我的心上。   Till it flowed into my heart.

我的心充满惆怅，   My heart was filled with sorrow,

不为那弯弯的月亮，   Not for that hook of crescent,

只为那今天的村庄，   But for today's village,

还唱着过去的歌谣。   Which sings lullaby of yesterday.

哦……故乡的月亮，   Oh hometown crescent,

你那弯弯的忧伤，   With that arc of melancholy,

穿透了我的胸膛。   You pierce through my chest.

学唱中国歌

三 生词详解 (New words)

1. 遥远　　（形）　　yáoyuǎn　　remote
2. 夜空　　（名）　　yèkōng　　sky in the night
3. 下面　　（名）　　xiàmian　　underneath
4. 桥　　　（名）　　qiáo　　　bridge
5. 旁边　　（名）　　pángbiān　side
6. 船　　　（名）　　chuán　　boat
7. 悠悠　　（形）　　yōuyōu　　floating gently
8. 童年　　（名）　　tóngnián　childhood
9. 阿娇　　（人名）　Ā jiāo　　*Ajiao*, a girl's name
10. 摇　　　（动）　　yáo　　　row
11. 唱　　　（动）　　chàng　　sing
12. 古老　　（形）　　gǔlǎo　　ancient
13. 歌谣　　（名）　　gēyáo　　lullaby
14. 随　　　（动）　　suí　　　to move with
15. 风　　　（名）　　fēng　　 wind
16. 淌　　　（动）　　tǎng　　 flow down, shed (tears)
17. 河水　　（名）　　héshuǐ　 river
18. 流　　　（动）　　liú　　　flow
19. 充满　　（动）　　chōngmǎn　to fill up
20. 惆怅　　（形）　　chóuchàng　sorrow
21. 村庄　　（名）　　cūnzhuāng　village
22. 故乡　　（名）　　gùxiāng　　hometown
23. 忧伤　　（形）　　yōushāng　blue, sorrowful
24. 穿透　　　　　　　chuāntòu　pierce
25. 胸膛　　（名）　　xiōngtáng　chest

学唱中国歌

四 歌曲欣赏 (Music sheet)

弯弯的月亮

学唱中国歌

五 读一读 (Read the Following Passage)

中国人的月亮 The Chinese Moon

在中国传统文化中,有关月亮的神话传说、诗词比比皆是。民间很早就有赏月的传统习俗,流传着许多关于月亮的传说,比如"嫦娥奔月"、"吴刚伐桂"、"玉兔捣药"等等。一边赏月一边赋诗更是文人雅士的重要活动之一。

月亮在中国诗人的心中有着多种不同的含义:幽美、自由、纯洁、美好、永恒、凄凉、悲伤、思念等,人世间的悲欢离合都可以用月亮来表达。圆月如盘,象征团圆和幸福;残月如钩,象征残缺和离别。月亮圆了又缺,缺了又圆,人们在望月的时候,总会情不自禁地想念远游在外、客居异乡的亲人。远方的游子当然更忍不住思念故乡和亲人,如:"举头望明月,低头思故乡。"(李白《静夜思》)如:"人有悲欢离合,月有阴晴圆缺,此事古难全,但愿人长久,千里共婵娟。"(苏轼《水调歌头》)月亮也可以用来表达情人间的思念与怨恨,如:"恨君不似江楼月,南北东西,南北东西,只有相随无别离。恨君却似江楼月,暂满还亏,暂满还亏,待得团圆是几时?"(吕本中《采桑子》)《月儿弯弯照九州》这首歌中唱到的"月儿弯弯照几州,几家欢乐几家愁",其实也是借月牙儿的残缺来比喻夫妻别离、孤苦飘零。

在中国传统文化中,月亮是诗意的月亮,是饱含情感的月亮。

In Chinese traditional culture, the moon is often mentioned in legends, myths, and poems, and it is a popular custom for people to admire the moon. Tales related to the moon that are frequently told include "Chang'e Flies to the Moon", "Wu Gang Chops Laurel Trees", and "Jade Rabbit Pounding Herbs in a Mortar".

学唱中国歌

Intellectuals often get inspired and write poems when appreciating the moon.

The moon has many different symbolic meanings in the mind of Chinese poets, for example beauty of loneliness, freedom, purity, nicety, consistency, desolation, sorrow, yearning for someone, etc. It seems that many events in the human society, like getting together, parting, happiness, and sadness can all be expressed with the help of the moon. A full moon symbolizes togetherness and happiness; a crescent moon represents incompleteness and separation. People watch the moon wax and wane and think about their relatives who are far away from home. For those who are traveling, the moon will also remind them of their home and family. We have a whole collection of poems about that theme.

Raising my head I see the bright moon;
Lowering down my head I think of my hometown.

Li Bai, "Thoughts on a Silent Night"

People may have happiness or sorrow, are together or apart.
The moon also waxes and wanes.
It has been like this since the ancient times.
I wish we're always there for each other.
We enjoy the same moon though we're thousands of miles apart.

Su Shi, "Shui Diao Ge tou"

The image of the moon in poetry is also used to express passion and sorrowful hate between lovers.
Why are you not like the moon?
Moving only from one side to the other in the sky,
So that you're always with me and we never part.

学唱中国歌

And how come you're just like the moon?
Being full just for a short time,
Letting me wait for so long to be together with you.

Lu Benzhong, "Cai Sang Zi"

There are lyrics like "The crescent moon is shining over China, how many families are happy? And how many are in agony?" in the song "Crescent Moon over China", in which the crescent is used metaphorically as an image of parted couple's lonely and drifting life.

In traditional Chinese culture, the moon is the moon of poetry and the moon of sentiment.

六 说一说 (Ask and Answer)

1. 故乡的哪幅画面浮现在作者的脑海里?
2. 今天的村庄"还唱着过去的歌谣"是什么意思?
3. 解释"人有悲欢离合,月有阴晴圆缺,此事古难全"这一句的意思。
4. 在你的国家,有没有关于月亮的神话传说。

七 做一做 (Tasks)

1. "床前明月光"是哪首诗中的句子? 作者是谁?
2. 查找中国有关月亮的传说故事。

八 词语链接 (Related Words or Phrases)

1. 曲调　　(名)　　qǔdiào　　　　tune

学唱中国歌

2. 优美　　（形）　yōuměi　　　　graceful, exquisite
3. 思乡　　（动）　sīxiāng　　　　to think of one's home, to be homesick
4. 主人公　（名）　zhǔréngōng　　protagonist
5. 回忆　　（动）　huíyì　　　　　recollect
6. 岁月匆匆　　　　suìyuè cōngcōng　time flies
7. 朦胧　　（形）　ménglóng　　　dusky, hazy
8. 往事　　（名）　wǎngshì　　　　the bygones
9. 浮现　　（动）　fúxiàn　　　　　emerge (in one's mind)
10. 脑海　　（名）　nǎohǎi　　　　mind

学唱中国歌

11 常回家看看
Come Back Home Often

一 推荐絮语 (Introduction)

《常回家看看》(车行作词,戚建波作曲)是一首轻松活泼、欢乐祥和、饱含着浓浓的亲情的歌曲。歌词朴实直白,但这种非常生活化的语言却以一种巨大的亲和力,唱出了老百姓的心里话,表现了儿女和父母渴望团聚的亲情,引起人们的共鸣,打动了很多老人和儿女的心。

Come Back Home Often (lyrics by Che Xing, music by Qi Jianbo) is a lively, auspicious song and sings about affection among family members. The lyrics are frank and straightforward, but those exact words we use in daily life show great affinity. It is sung from ordinary people's hearts, a song about the aspiration of family members to be together, which expresses the deep-felt feeling of many parents and children.

二 歌词对读 (Chinese and English lyrics)

zhǎo diǎn kòngxián, zhǎo diǎn shí jiān
找点空闲,找点时间,
When you are free and have time,

lǐng zhe hái zi, cháng huí jiā kàn kan
领着孩子,常回家看看。
Take your children and visit your parents' home often.

学唱中国歌

dài shàng xiào róng, dài shàng zhù fú 带上笑容，带上祝福，	Bring your smile and heart-felt wishes,
péi tóng ài rén cháng huí jiā kàn kan 陪同爱人常回家看看。	Take your loved one and visit your parents' home often.
mā ma zhǔn bèi le yī xiē láo dao 妈妈准备了一些唠叨；	Mama has prepared some chatter,
bà ba zhāng luo le yī zhuō hǎo fàn 爸爸张罗了一桌好饭。	Papa is ready with a table of delicious food.
shēng huó de fán nǎo gēn mā ma shuō shuo 生活的烦恼跟妈妈说说；	Talk to mother about troubles in life,
gōng zuò de shì qing gēn bà ba tán tan 工作的事情跟爸爸谈谈。	Discuss with Papa issues in work.
cháng huí jiā kàn kan, huí jiā kàn kan 常回家看看，回家看看，	Come back home often, come back home often,
nǎ pà bāng mā ma shuā shuā kuài zi 哪怕帮妈妈刷刷筷子、 xǐ xi wǎn 洗洗碗，	Even just to help with washing the dishes.
lǎo rén bù tú ér nǚ wèi jiā zuò duō 老人不图儿女为家做多 dà gòng xiàn 大贡献。	Parents don't expect a lot from children,
yī bèi zi bù róng yì jiù tú gè tuán tuán 一辈子不容易就图个团团 yuán yuán 圆圆！	After life-long hard work they just want the family to be together.
cháng huí jiā kàn kan, huí jiā kàn kan 常回家看看，回家看看，	Come back home often, come back home often,

学唱中国歌

nǎ pà gěi bà ba chuí chui hòu bèi
哪怕给爸爸捶捶后背、 Even just to stroke Papa's back and
róu rou jiān
揉揉肩， give him a massage.
lǎo rén bù tú ér nǚ wèi jiā zuò
老人不图儿女为家做 Parents don't expect a lot from
duō dà gòngxiàn
多大贡献。 children,
yī bèi zi zǒng cāo xīn jiù bèn gè
一辈子总操心就奔个 After life-long hard work they just want
píngpíng ān ān
平平安安。 the family to be peaceful and safe.

三 生词详解 (New words)

1. 常　　（副）　　cháng　　often
2. 回　　（动）　　huí　　return, come back
3. 空闲　（名、动）　kòngxián　free time
4. 时间　（名）　　shíjiān　　time
5. 孩子　（名）　　háizi　　kid, child
6. 笑容　（名）　　xiàoróng　smile
7. 陪同　（动）　　péitóng　　accompany
8. 妈妈　（名）　　māma　　mama
9. 准备　（动）　　zhǔnbèi　　prepare
10. 唠叨　（动）　　láodao　　chatter
11. 爸爸　（名）　　bàba　　papa
12. 张罗　（动）　　zhāngluo　take care of, get busy about
13. 桌　　（量、名）　zhuō　　table
14. 饭　　（名）　　fàn　　food, meal
15. 生活　（名、动）　shēnghuó　life

学唱中国歌

16.	跟	（介）	gēn	with
17.	工作	（名、动）	gōngzuò	work
18.	事情	（名）	shìqing	thing, issue
19.	谈	（动）	tán	talk
20.	刷	（动）	shuā	wash (dishes), scrub
21.	筷子	（名）	kuàizi	chopstick
22.	洗	（动）	xǐ	wash
23.	碗	（名）	wǎn	bowl
24.	图	（动）	tú	intend
25.	为	（介）	wèi	for
26.	做	（动）	zuò	do
27.	贡献	（名、动）	gòngxiàn	contribution
28.	容易	（形）	róngyì	easy
29.	锤	（动）	chuí	thump, pound
30.	后背	（名）	hòubèi	back
31.	揉	（动）	róu	rub
32.	肩	（名）	jiān	shoulder
33.	操心		cāo xīn	worry about, be concerned over
34.	奔	（动）	bèn	be busy running about, work hard to get something

学唱中国歌

四 歌曲欣赏 (Music sheet)

常回家看看

学唱中国歌

五 读一读 (Read the Following Passage)

孝 Filial Piety

中国人最重孝道,一直有"百善孝为先"的说法。孝是中国几千年传统固有的美德,也是中国社会道德的基石。

中国传统孝道的精髓在于提倡对父母的"敬"和"爱"。孔子曾说:"今之孝者,是谓能养。至于犬马,皆能有养,不敬,何以别乎?"意思是,对待父母不仅仅是物质供养,关键在于要有对父母的爱,而且这种爱是发自内心的真爱。没有这种爱,不仅谈不上对父母孝敬,而且和饲养犬马没有什么两样。

除了在生活和精神上精心照顾老人外,孝的内容还包括"立身"和"谏诤"。"立身"是指子女在工作中取得了成绩,使父母为自己感到光荣,由此使他们心情愉快,这也是一种孝。"谏诤"是指对父母不能盲目顺从,如果发现父母有做错的地方,子女也应该指出来,帮助他们改正。

Chinese people always put filial piety as their first priority. There is a saying which goes "Of the one hundred merits of a man, filial piety comes first." It is a virtue that has been valued by the Chinese all through its several-thousand-year-long civilization, and serves as the cornerstone of Chinese social ethics.

The essence of Chinese filial piety is the promotion of respect and love for the parents. Confucius once said, "今之孝者,是谓能养。至于犬马,皆能有养,不敬,何以别乎?" which means the right way to treat one's parents is not just to support them materially, but to love and care about them, and this love should come from one's heart. Without such love, one's support for parents is just like keeping animals like dogs and horses, and could

学唱中国歌

not be called filial piety.

Besides supporting the elderly materially and psychologically, there are other aspects like "*lishen*" and "*jianzheng*" in the Chinese filial piety. *Lishen* means to make achievements in work and make parents feel proud and happy. *Jianzheng* means to not follow parents' instructions blindly, i.e. when the parents make mistakes, children should point them out and help parents correct them.

六 说一说 (Ask and Answer)

1. 你和父母住在一起吗？常回家看望他们吗？
2. 怎么理解歌中的"生活的烦恼跟妈妈说说，工作的事情向爸爸谈谈"？
3. 根据歌曲，老人对儿女的希望是什么？
4. 你怎么理解"孝"？

七 做一做 (Tasks)

1. 你认为孩子结婚后和父母住在一起好还是分开住好？
2. 介绍一下你的国家子女与父母的关系，并查找相关资料。

八 词语链接 (Related Words or Phrases)

1. 轻松	（形）	qīngsōng	relaxed
2. 活泼	（形）	huópō	lively
3. 生活化		shēnghuóhuà	being close to daily life
4. 渴望	（动）	kěwàng	aspire, desire

学唱中国歌

5.	引起	（动）	yǐnqǐ	evoke
6.	共鸣	（名）	gòngmíng	resonance
7.	打动	（动）	dǎdòng	move, touch, arouse one's feelings
8.	孝	（名、动）	xiào	filial piety, treat parents with filial piety
9.	美德	（名）	měidé	virtue
10.	精髓	（名）	jīngsuǐ	marrow, pith

学唱中国歌

12 青藏高原
Tibetan Plateau

一 推荐絮语 (Introduction)

《青藏高原》(张千一作词作曲)是电视连续剧《天路》的主题歌,这是一首把少数民族音乐与流行音乐成功地结合在一起的歌曲,歌曲旋律明亮高亢,藏族山歌风格的长调体现出青藏高原的古老和庄严。

Tibetan Plateau (lyrics and music by Zhang Qianyi) is the theme music of the TV series *Road to Heaven*. This is a song which successfully combined the elements of minority ethnic group music and pop music. The bright and sonorous tone combined with the Tibetan folk music style reveals the image of an ancient and solemn plateau.

二 歌词对读 (Chinese and English lyrics)

yā lā suǒ āi　　shì shéi dài lái yuǎn gǔ de
呀啦索哎,是谁带来远古的
hū huàn
呼唤?

(Ya-la-so-ei) Who brought the call from the ancient time?

shì shuí liú xià qiānnián de qí pàn
是谁留下千年的祈盼?

And left the prayer one thousand years behind?

学唱中国歌

nán dào shuō hái yǒu wú yán de gē 难道说还有无言的歌，	Is it true that there is a wordless song,
hái shi nà jiǔ jiǔ bù néng wàng huái de juàn liàn 还是那久久不能忘怀的眷恋。	Or it is just a sentimental feeling that cannot be forgotten.
ó wǒ kàn jiàn yī zuò zuò shān yī zuò zuò 哦，我看见一座座山一座座 shān chuān 山川，	Oh, I can see those mountains,
yī zuò zuò shān chuān xiāng lián 一座座山川相连，	Mountains after mountains,
ya lā suǒ nà kě shì qīngzàng gāo yuán 呀啦索，那可是青藏高原？	(ya-la-so) Is it the Tibetan Plateau?
shì shuí rì yè yáo wàng zhe lán tiān 是谁日夜遥望着蓝天？	Day and night, who looks into the sky?
shì shuí kě wàng yǒng jiǔ de mèng huàn 是谁渴望永久的梦幻？	Who dreams of the ultimate fantasy?
nán dào shuō hái yǒu zàn měi de gē 难道说还有赞美的歌，	Is it true that there is a song of praising,
hái shi nà fǎng fú bù néng gǎi biàn de zhuāng yán 还是那仿佛不能改变的庄严。	Or it is the solemnity that cannot be changed.
ó wǒ kàn jiàn yī zuò zuò shān yī zuò zuò 哦，我看见一座座山一座座 shān chuān 山川，	Oh, I can see those mountains,
yī zuò zuò shān chuān xiāng lián 一座座山川相连，	Mountains after mountains,

学唱中国歌

> yā lā suǒ, nà jiù shì qīng zàng gāo yuán
> 呀啦索,那就是青藏高原。(Ya-la-so) Is it the Tibetan Plateau?

三 生词详解 (New words)

1. 青藏高原	(专名)	Qīng-Zàng gāoyuán	Tibetan Plateau, Qinghai-Tibetan Plateau
2. 谁	(代)	shuí	who
3. 远古	(名)	yuǎngǔ	ancient times
4. 呼唤	(名、动)	hūhuàn	call
5. 留下	(动)	liúxià	leave
6. 祈盼	(动)	qípàn	pray for and expect
7. 难道	(连)	nándào	Is it possible that...?
8. 无言		wúyán	without any words
9. 歌	(名)	gē	song
10. 久久	(副)	jiǔjiǔ	for a long time
11. 不能		bùnéng	cannot
12. 忘怀	(动)	wànghuái	forget
13. 眷恋	(动)	juànliàn	be sentimentally attached to (a person or a place)
14. 座	(量)	zuò	measure word for mountain and hill
15. 山川	(名)	shānchuān	mountains and rivers
16. 相连	(动)	xiānglián	connect, link
17. 可	(副、连)	kě	used to emphasize a rhetorical question
18. 日夜	(名)	rìyè	day and night

学唱中国歌

19. 遥望　（动）　yáowàng　to look at something from distance
20. 永久　（形）　yǒngjiǔ　permanent
21. 梦幻　（名）　mènghuàn　dream, fantasy
22. 赞美　（动）　zànměi　praise
23. 仿佛　（动）　fǎngfú　as if, like
24. 庄严　（形）　zhuāngyán　solemn

四 歌曲欣赏 (Music sheet)

青藏高原

学唱中国歌

学唱中国歌

五 读一读 (Read the Following Passage)

青藏高原 Tibetan Plateau

青藏高原是世界上最高的高原,平均海拔高度在4000米以上,有"世界屋脊"和"地球第三极"之称。

青藏高原的总面积为250万平方公里,包括中国西藏自治区、青海省的全部和新疆维吾尔自治区、甘肃省、四川省、云南省的一部分,以及中国的邻国不丹、尼泊尔、印度、巴基斯坦、阿富汗、塔吉克斯坦、吉尔吉斯斯坦的部分或全部。

青藏高原上人烟稀少,空气干燥稀薄,太阳辐射比较强,气温低,降雨比较少。尽管气候条件恶劣,但这里在两万年前的旧石器时期就已经有人类生存了。勤劳勇敢的藏族和其他民族的人民世代居住在青藏高原上,他们的文化受到其周围文化(汉文化、西域文化和印度文化)的影响,但同时它也保存了自己的独特性。

The Tibetan Plateau, with an average elevation of over 4,000 meters, is the highest plateau in the world and known as "the roof of the world" and "the third Pole".

Covering an area of 2,500,000 square kilometers, the Tibetan Plateau refers to the vast area including Tibet Autonomous Region and Qinghai Province in China, part of Xinjiang Uyghur Autonomous Region, Gansu Province, Sichuan Province, Yunnan Province, and part or all of neighboring countries like Bhutan, Nepal, India, Pakistan, Afghanistan, Tadzhikistan, and Kyrgyzstan.

This area is sparsely populated. The air above the plateau is so thin and dry that it cannot resist much of the solar radiation. The temperature on the plateau is low with little precipitation. Though climate is dreadful there, there have been traces of humans from as early as the Old Stone Age (20,000 years ago). The brave and hardworking

学唱中国歌

Tibetan people have been living on the plateau for so long and their culture managed to stay unique while receiving influence from the surrounding civilizations like Han, Western, and Indian.

六 说一说 (Ask and Answer)

1. 西藏为什么被称为"世界屋脊"？
2. 青藏高原的面积有多大？包括中国的哪几个省？
3. 有哪些国家位于青藏高原上？
4. 青藏高原的气候条件怎么样？

七 做一做 (Tasks)

1. 世界上最高的山在哪个国家，叫什么山？海拔高度是多少？
2. 你知道中国的青藏铁路吗？查找并介绍相关情况。

八 词语链接 (Glossary)

1. 旋律	（名）	xuánlǜ	melody
2. 高亢	（形）	gāokàng	loud and sonorous
3. 藏族	（名）	Zàngzú	Tibetan
4. 庄严	（形）	zhuāngyán	solemn
5. 平均	（形、动）	píngjūn	balanced
6. 海拔	（名）	hǎibá	altitude
7. 面积	（名）	miànjī	area
8. 人烟稀少		rényān xīshǎo	sparsely-populated
9. 干燥	（形）	gānzào	dry
10. 勤劳	（形）	qínláo	diligent

学唱中国歌

13 雾里看花
Flower in Mist

一 推荐絮语 (Introduction)

生活中假的东西太多了，不仅仅是商品，还有假话、假仁假义等等，人们都渴望有一双"慧眼"，能够把一切"看得清清楚楚明明白白真真切切"。《雾里看花》(阎肃作词，孙川作曲)这首歌正是写出了人们对"真"的渴望，而正是这种渴望，使得歌曲深入人心、留在了人们的记忆中。

Too many things in life are fake: commodities, words, and pretended kindness. Everyone wants to have a pair of perceptive eyes, which can see things clearly, explicitly and vividly. *Flower in Mist* (lyrics by Yan Su, music by Sun Chuan) is a song about people's craving for truth. The song remains in people's memory for a long time because this craving is common.

二 歌词对读 (Chinese and English lyrics)

wù lǐ kàn huā　shuǐ zhōng wàng yuè
雾里看花，水中望月，

Flower in the mist, moon in the water,

nǐ néng fēn biàn zhè biàn huàn mò cè de shì jiè
你能分辨这变幻莫测的世界？

Can you understand the unpredictable world?

学唱中国歌

<tāo zǒu yún fēi, huā kāi huā xiè>
涛走云飞，花开花谢，

<nǐ néng bǎ wò zhè yáo yè duō zī de jì jié>
你能把握这摇曳多姿的季节？

<fán nǎo zuì shì wú qíng yè>
烦恼最是无情夜，

<xiào yǔ huān yán, nán dào shuō nà jiù shì qīn rè>
笑语欢颜，难道说那就是亲热？

<wēn cún wèi bì jiù shì tǐ tiē>
温存未必就是体贴，

<nǐ zhī nǎ jù shì zhēn nǎ jù shì jiǎ>
你知哪句是真哪句是假？

<nǎ yī jù shì qíng sī níng jié>
哪一句是情丝凝结？

<jiè wǒ jiè wǒ yī shuāng huì yǎn ba>
借我借我一双慧眼吧，

<ràng wǒ bǎ zhè fēn rǎo>
让我把这纷扰，

<kàn de qīngqing chǔ chu míngming bái bai>
看得清清楚楚明明白白

<zhēnzhen qiè qie>
真真切切。

Like the wave will move and cloud will fly away, the blooming flower will also wither and fall so,

Can you comprehend the flickering flickering and colourful season?

The most annoying is a heartless night,

When one feels no affection even surrounded by laughters and smiles?

Tenderness does not necessarily mean care,

How do you know which word is true and which is fake?

Which is the expression of real emotion?

Lend me a pair of piercing eyes,

Let me see through the chaos,

Clearly, explicitly and vividly.

学唱中国歌

三 生词详解(New words)

1. 雾　　　　(名)　　wù　　　　　　　mist
2. 望　　　　(动)　　wàng　　　　　　look from a distance
3. 分辨　　　(动)　　fēnbiàn　　　　 differentiate
4. 变幻莫测　　　　　biànhuàn mòcè　 unpredictably changing
5. 世界　　　(名)　　shìjiè　　　　　world
6. 涛　　　　(名)　　tāo　　　　　　 waves
7. 花开花落　　　　　huā kāi huā luò flowers bloom and then wither
8. 把握　　　(动)　　bǎwò　　　　　　grasp, control
9. 摇曳多姿　　　　　yáoyè duōzī　　 shaking slightly in many carriages
10. 季节　　 (名)　　jìjié　　　　　 season
11. 无情　　 (形)　　wúqíng　　　　　heartless
12. 笑语　　 (名)　　xiàoyǔ　　　　　talking and laughing
13. 欢颜　　 (名)　　huānyán　　　　 smiling face, delighted face
14. 亲热　　 (形、动)　qīnrè　　　　 intimate, warm-hearted
15. 未必　　 (副)　　wèibì　　　　　 not necessarily
16. 体贴　　 (动)　　tǐtiē　　　　　 considerate, caring
17. 句　　　 (量、名)　jù　　　　　　sentence
18. 假　　　 (形)　　jiǎ　　　　　　 fake
19. 情丝　　 (名)　　qíngsī　　　　　threads of affection or emotion
20. 凝结　　 (动)　　níngjié　　　　 condense
21. 慧眼　　 (名)　　huìyǎn　　　　　piercing eye

学唱中国歌

22. 纷扰	（形）	fēnrǎo	chaos
23. 清楚	（形）	qīngchu	clear
24. 明白	（形、动）	míngbái	clear, explicit
25. 真切	（形）	zhēnqiè	vivid

四 歌曲欣赏 (Music sheet)

雾里看花

雾里看花，水中望月， 你能分辨这变幻莫测的世界？
烦恼最是无情夜， 笑语欢颜，难道说那就是亲热？

涛走云飞，花开花谢，你能把握这摇曳多姿的季节？
温存未必就是体贴，

你知哪句是真 哪句是假？哪 一句是情 丝

凝 结？ 借我借我一双慧眼吧，让我

把这纷扰，看得清清楚楚明明白白真真切切。

学唱中国歌

借我借我一双慧眼吧,让我把这纷扰,看得清清楚楚明明白白真真切切。

五 读一读 (Read the Following Passage)

张大千仿画 Zhang Daqian and his "Counterfeit Paintings"

在古物市场上,赝品是屡见不鲜的。所谓赝品是指伪造、仿制的物品。收藏古代文物、字画的人最怕遇到这些以假乱真的赝品。因此对古代文物的鉴定,是一门专门的学问,世界各国都设立了专门的机构。

在中国书画界,大部分人在学画时往往要先临摹前辈名家的画作,揣摩名家用笔、用墨的方法技巧、构图特点及表现神韵等。有些人由于长期模仿,仿作甚至达到了与真迹极为近似的水平。

张大千是中国现代一位著名的国画大师,可是却很少有人知道,这样一位艺术巨匠年轻时竟是模仿名作、绘制赝品的高手。在成名之前,被人们称奇的不是他创作的作品,而是他模仿明末清初画家石涛而作的赝品。张大千曾自嘲地说自己是个用纸用笔的骗子。他仿石涛画的赝品在神韵、表现手法、构图特点上惟妙惟肖,与真迹毫无二致,简直可以说是"石涛复生"。

张大千的仿画可以乱真,令鉴赏家们伤透了脑筋,丢尽了面子。但他师古而不泥古,学习古人的画法画意,融会贯通,终于成为享誉海内外的中国画一代宗师。

In antique market, collectors after encounter fakes, which are imitations made in an attempt to deceptively represent its origins. In order to avoid this kind of misfortune, collectors of antiques, paintings, or calligraphies have developed a special field of study: counterfeit detection. Countries all over the world have also established institutions to identify the fake antiques.

In China, when people learn to paint, most of them will imitate the works of famous painters so that they can experience and eventually master the skills. Some people, because they have been imitating other people's paintings for so long, develop really good skills, and their counterfeits can't be distinguished from the genuine article.

Zhang Daqian, the most famous modern Chinese painter, was known as "the best of the recent 500 years". But very few people know this master of Chinese art used to be a genius of counterfeiting. Before he became famous as a painter himself, he was known for his "work" of imitation of the Qing dynasty painter Shi Tao. Zhang used to say self-mockingly that he was a deceiver of paper and brush. Actually, the fakes he made are so like the original in style and charm, painting skills, and composition that he could be called "Shi Tao who was reborn".

Zhang Daqian's counterfeits have made great trouble and caused embarrassment to the art specialists. While Zhang was learning from people before him, he was free of the fetters of old works. He learned old painters' skills and experience of painting, and blended them harmoniously while developing his own style out of it. And that was how he became THE painter of Chinese modern times.

学唱中国歌

六 说一说 (Ask and Answer)

1. 歌曲中"雾里看花"和"水中望月"是指什么？
2. 你怎么理解"温存未必就是体贴"这句话？
3. 人们为什么渴望有"一双慧眼"？
4. 在生活中,你遇到过假货吗？举例说一说。

七 做一做 (Tasks)

1. "慧眼"本来是佛教术语,它的本意是什么？
2. 查找中国有关打击假冒产品的资料。

八 词语链接 (Related Words or Phrases)

1.	伪造	（动） wěizào	counterfeit
2.	仿制	（动） fǎngzhì	copy, imitate
3.	以假乱真	yǐ jiǎ luàn zhēn	mix the spurious with the genuine
4.	赝品	（名） yànpǐn	fake
5.	文物	（名） wénwù	cultural or historical relics
6.	鉴定	（动） jiàndìng	appraise
7.	临摹	（动） línmó	copy, imitate (the famous artwork)
8.	模仿	（动） mófǎng	imitate
9.	真迹	（名） zhēnjì	authentic work
10.	惟妙惟肖	wéi miào wéi xiào	be absolutely lifelike

学唱中国歌

14 阳光总在风雨后

After Storms There Always Comes Sunshine

一 推荐絮语 (Introduction)

人生的道路坎坷而漫长,有着风风雨雨,迎接你的不可能总是阳光和鲜花。只要你"跌倒"后不放弃,"风雨"中不退缩,勇敢地抬头向前,就一定会尝到成功的喜悦,因为"坚持就是胜利"。《阳光总在风雨后》(陈佳明作词,吴庆隆作曲)用歌曲的形式唱出了这一人生哲理:只有经历风雨,才能见到最美丽的彩虹。

Life is a long road filled with hardship and toil, just like rain and wind in a storm. It is not possible that what greets you is always sunshine and flowers. As long as you do not give up even when you fall down, and do not retreat in the storm and stride forward with your head held up high, one day you will taste the sweet success, because "to persist is to win". *After Storm There Always Comes Sunshine* (lyrics by Chen Jiaming, music by Wu Qinglong) tells about the truth in life: Survive the storm and you will see the most beautiful rainbow.

二 歌词对读 (Chinese and English lyrics)

rén shēng lù shàng tián kǔ hé xǐ yōu
人生路上甜苦和喜忧, In life one goes through bitter and sweet, ups and downs,

学唱中国歌

<table>
<tr><td>

yuàn yì yǔ nǐ fēn dān suǒ yǒu
愿意与你分担所有。

nán miǎn céng jīng diē dǎo hé děng hòu
难免曾经跌倒和等候，

yào yǒng gǎn de tái tóu
要勇敢地抬头。

shuí yuàn cáng duǒ zài bì fēng de gǎng kǒu
谁愿藏躲在避风的港口，

nìng yǒu bō tāo xiōng yǒng de zì yóu
宁有波涛汹涌的自由。

yuàn shì nǐ xīn zhōng dēng tǎ de shǒu hòu
愿是你心中灯塔的守候，

zài mí wù zhōng ràng nǐ kàn tòu
在迷雾中让你看透。

yáng guāng zǒng zài fēng yǔ hòu
阳光总在风雨后，

wū yún shàng yǒu qíng kōng
乌云上有晴空。

zhēn xī suǒ yǒu de gǎn dòng
珍惜所有的感动，

</td><td>

And I would like to share them all with you.

Sometimes it is not possible to avoid times when you fall and can't go on,

Bravely, you should raise your head.

Who wants to just hide in the haven,

One usually choose to enjoy the freedom going into the stormy sea.

I hope I am waiting as the lighthouse in your heart,

And guide your way through the heavy fog.

Sunshine always comes after the storm,

Over the clouds there is sunny sky.

Cherish each little time when we get touched,

</td></tr>
</table>

学唱中国歌

_{měi yí fèn xī wàng zài nǐ shǒu zhōng}
每一份希望在你手中。   Every piece of hope is within your grasp.

_{yáng guāng zǒng zài fēng yǔ hòu}
阳光总在风雨后，   Sunshine always comes after the storm,

_{qǐng xiāng xìn yǒu cǎi hóng}
请相信有彩虹。   Please believe there will be rainbows.

_{fēng fēng yǔ yǔ dōu jiē shòu}
风风雨雨都接受，   No matter what kind of storm we will go through together,

_{wǒ yì zhí huì zài nǐ de zuǒ yòu}
我一直会在你的左右。   I'll always be with you.

三 生词详解 (New words)

1.	苦	（名）	kǔ	bitter
2.	喜	（名）	xǐ	happiness
3.	忧	（名）	yōu	sorrow
4.	分担	（动）	fēndān	share (responsibility)
5.	难免	（动）	nánmiǎn	cannot be avoided
6.	跌倒	（动）	diēdǎo	fall over
7.	等候	（动）	děnghòu	wait
8.	勇敢	（形）	yǒnggǎn	brave
9.	藏躲	（动）	cángduǒ	hide
10.	避风	（动）	bìfēng	to take shelter from the wind
11.	港口	（名）	gǎngkǒu	harbour
12.	宁愿	（副）	nìngyuàn	would rather

学唱中国歌

13. 波涛（名） bōtāo strong wave
14. 汹涌（形） xiōngyǒng surging, turbulent
15. 自由（名、形） zìyóu free
16. 灯塔（名） dēngtǎ lighthouse
17. 迷雾（名） míwù dense fog
18. 看透（动） kàntòu to gain insight into
19. 乌云（名） wūyún black cloud
20. 晴空（名） qíngkōng clear sky
21. 珍惜（动） zhēnxī cherish
22. 彩虹（名） cǎihóng rainbow
23. 风雨（名） fēngyǔ wind and rain, storm, hardship
24. 接受（动） jiēshòu accept
25. 左右（名） zuǒyòu left and right, be by one's side

四 歌曲欣赏 (Music sheet)

阳光总在风雨后

学唱中国歌

五 读一读 (Read the Following Passage)

和"风雨"有关的成语 Idioms of "Wind" and "Rain"

成语是人们长期以来习用的、简洁精辟的固定词语,主要来源于古代寓言、历史故事、文学作品和民间口语等,大多是四字结构。汉语成语的特点是意义完整、结构定型、表现力强。有些成语含有比喻义,不能只从字面上理解它的意思,比如下面关于"风雨"的成语。

1. 风吹雨打:指遭受风吹雨淋,多比喻恶势力对弱小者的迫害。
2. 风调雨顺:风雨适时适量,借指农作物获得丰收。
3. 风雨交加:指大风和暴雨一起袭来,有时比喻几种灾难一起袭来。
4. 风雨飘摇:指随着狂风和暴雨不停地摇晃,比喻社会动荡不安或局势摇摇欲坠。
5. 凄风苦雨:指寒冷的风,成灾的雨,形容天气恶劣,比喻处境悲惨凄凉。
6. 风雨同舟:指在风雨中同乘一条船渡河,比喻共度难关。
7. 风雨无阻:指刮风下雨也阻挡不了,比喻无论发生什么情况都照常进行。
8. 风雨兼程:指冒着风雨加倍赶路,比喻不受气候环境的影响,不停赶路。

An idiom is a fixed usage of phrase, which is usually brief and meaningful. Its origin may be from old fables, historical stories, literature works, or slang. Most Chinese idioms consist of four characters. Chinese idioms usually have accomplished meanings, fixed structures and powerful expression. Some idioms are metaphorical, the meaning of which cannot be deduced just from their literal definitions. Following are some example of "wind" and "rain" idioms.

1. *Feng chui yu da*: being exposed in wind and rain; the weak bullied by the evil and strong
2. *Feng tiao yu shun*: suitable amount of wind and rain; favorable weather for the crops
3. *Feng yu jiao jia*: raining and blowing hard; hit by several disasters at the same time
4. *Feng yu piao yao*: being blown and shaken in the strong wind and rain; unstable social situation or a shaky government
5. *Qi feng ku yu*: cold wind and disastrous rain; dreadful climate; (a person) being in a miserable situation
6. *Feng yu tong zhou*: traveling in one boat through wind and rain; stand together through difficulty
7. *Feng yu wu zu*: won't be stopped by wind or rain; to do something as scheduled no matter what happens
8. *Feng yu jian cheng*: to travel with double speed in wind and rain; to go one's way without being affected by the surroundings

六 说一说 (Ask and Answer)

1. 歌曲中的"阳光"、"风雨"、"乌云"和"彩虹"各借指什么？
2. "跌倒和等候"是指什么？
3. "藏躲在避风的港口"是指什么？
4. "风风雨雨都接受"是指什么？

七 做一做 (Tasks)

1. 在你的生活中有哪些难忘的"甜苦和喜忧"？

学唱中国歌

2. "灯塔"是什么？介绍你的国家有关风雨等的象征说法。

八 词语链接 (Related Words or Phrases)

1. 坎坷	（名）	kǎnkě	trail, hardship
2. 漫长	（形）	màncháng	very long, endless
3. 挫折	（名）	cuòzhé	frustration
4. 放弃	（动）	fàngqì	give up
5. 退缩	（动）	tuìsuō	retreat, shrink back
6. 坚持	（动）	jiānchí	persist
7. 胜利	（名）	shènglì	victory
8. 哲理	（名）	zhélǐ	philosophy
9. 无奈	（动）	wúnài	have no alternative
10. 喜悦	（名）	xǐyuè	delight, joy

学唱中国歌

15 一剪梅
A Spray of Plum Blossom

一 推荐絮语 (Introduction)

自古以来,赞美梅花的诗歌非常多,人们欣赏梅花在严冬来临、百花凋谢后,依然不惧严寒、傲雪挺立的品格。很多人曾提出将梅花和牡丹并列为中国的国花,可见梅花在中国人心中的地位。《一剪梅》(陈怡作词,娃娃作曲)是一首借梅花歌颂真情能够不畏风雪的歌,它的画面感很强,使人仿佛看到一朵梅花正迎着呼啸的寒风,独自在雪中开放。

Ever since ancient times, there have been many poems about plum blossoms in China. People admire its spirit of blooming in the most severe cold, even in snow. Many people nominated the plum flower as a candidate for the title of "national flower", alongside with peony, which shows the position of plum flower in the Chinese mentality. *A Spray of Plum Blossom* (lyrics by Chen Yi, Music by Wawa) is a song singing the praises of true love, which is like the plum flower that endures the intense cold and snow in winter. The song is very picturesque, providing people with a vivid image of a branch of plum flowers blooming alone in the roaring cold wind and falling snow.

学唱中国歌

二 歌词对读 (Chinese and English lyrics)

zhēn qíng xiàng cǎo yuán guǎng kuò 真情像草原广阔，	True love is like a vast grassland,
céng céng fēng yǔ bù néng zǔ gé 层层风雨不能阻隔，	That cannot be blocked by wind and rain,
zǒng yǒu yún kāi rì chū shí hou 总有云开日出时候，	There will always come a time when the sun comes out,
wàn zhàng yáng guāng zhào liàng nǐ wǒ 万丈阳光照亮你我。	And its beam will shine on me and you.
zhēn qíng xiàng méi huā kāi biàn 真情像梅花开遍，	True love is like a plum flower that has bloomed,
lěng lěng bīng xuě bù néng yān mò 冷冷冰雪不能淹没，	That cannot be devoured by ice and snow,
jiù zài zuì lěng zhī tóu zhàn fàng 就在最冷枝头绽放，	Blooming right on the spray in the most intense cold,
kàn jiàn chūn tiān zǒu xiàng nǐ wǒ 看见春天走向你我。	It is among the first to see the spring drawing near.
xuě huā piāo piāo běi fēng xiào xiào 雪花飘飘北风啸啸，	Snowflakes flying, north wind roaring,
tiān dì yí piàn cāng máng 天地一片苍茫，	The snow-covered earth is boundless,

学唱中国歌

> yī jiǎn hán méi ào lì xuě zhōng
> 一剪寒梅傲立雪中，
> With only the spray of plum flowers proudly blooming in the snow,
>
> zhǐ wèi yī rén piāo xiāng
> 只为伊人飘香。
> Sending out its scent just for you.
>
> ài wǒ suǒ ài wú yuàn wú huǐ
> 爱我所爱无怨无悔，
> Love my love and never regret,
>
> cǐ qíng cháng liú xīn jiān
> 此情长留心间。
> The love will always be in my heart.

三 生词详解 (New words)

1. 剪　　　　（名）　　jiǎn　　　　　cut (with scissors)
2. 真情　　　（名）　　zhēnqíng　　　true love, genuine feelings
3. 广阔　　　（形）　　guǎngkuò　　　broad, vast
4. 层层　　　（副）　　céngcéng　　　layers and layers of
5. 阻隔　　　（动）　　zǔgé　　　　　block, separate
6. 万丈　　　（数）　　wànzhàng　　　lofty or bottomless
7. 淹没　　　（动）　　yānmò　　　　submerge
8. 绽放　　　（动）　　zhànfàng　　　bloom
9. 啸啸　　　（拟声）　xiāoxiāo　　　(onomatopoeia) sound of the wind
10. 苍茫　　　（形）　　cāngmáng　　　vast and boundless
11. 傲立　　　（动）　　àolì　　　　　proudly stand
12. 伊人　　　（代）　　yīrén　　　　 that person (usu. a woman)
13. 爱我所爱　　　　　　ài wǒ suǒ ài　love my love
14. 无怨无悔　　　　　　wú yuàn wú huǐ　without any complaint or regret

学唱中国歌

15. 此　　（代）　　cǐ　　this

四 歌曲欣赏 (Music sheet)

一剪梅

95

学唱中国歌

五 读一读 (Read the Following Passage)

四君子 The Four Noble Ones

"君子"本来指品格高尚的人，但在中国人的精神世界里，梅、兰、竹、菊四种植物由于品性高洁而被称为"四君子"。

梅花的花朵虽然很小，然而它却能在冰天雪地中一枝独秀，代表了一种逆境下的勃勃生机，这种铁骨冰心的精神，正是中华民族精神的象征。

淡雅、素净的兰花生性清洁，不与杂草为伍，既可寄生于树上，又可生长于无土的石缝中，"幽香清远，神静韵高"，是"花中的君子"。

竹生长的速度很快，几年就可以成材，竹笋可食，竹器可用，在南方与百姓的生活极为密切。它的姿态挺拔秀颀，象征着高洁出众的气质；竹内虚心有节，象征着中国人的谦虚和操守。

陶渊明"采菊东篱下，悠然见南山"的诗句，使菊花成为淡泊名利、超然世外的象征。人们在百花凋零的秋季有不畏霜雪的菊花为伴，精神世界也就有了寄托之处。

"*Jun zi*" originally refer to those who have noble character. In the Chinese mentality, the plum blossom, the orchid, the bamboo, and the chrysanthemum are called "the four noble ones" because they represent admirable noble characters.

The plum blossom has very small flowers, and is the only bloomer in the ice and snow of winter. It represents vitality in adverse circumstances. This spirit of "iron bone and crystal heart" is an emblem of the spirit of the Chinese people.

Orchid, without any flashy colors or strong scent, does not choose to live among the weeds. It would rather grow by a tree

学唱中国歌

trunk or among rocks, where there is little soil. "Producing a mild scent that is elegant which can travel a long way, and holding an air so quiet and above the common ones", orchid is considered a "gentleman among flowers".

Bamboo can grow really fast and become usable timber in just a few years. A bamboo shoot can be eaten; bamboo crafts are also common in the southern Chinese's daily life. Bamboo grows tall and straight, and resembles outstandingly noble and virtuous character. Bamboo is hollow and has many joints (*jie*, which also means integrity in Chinese), and therefore is considered a symbol of modesty and moral courage, which is valued by the Chinese.

Tao Yuanming once wrote in his poem: "I pluck chrysanthemums under the eastern hedge, and then gaze afar towards the southern hills." From then on, the chrysanthemum has become an icon of being indifferent to fame and fortune. Accompanied by the chrysanthemum blooming in the season when other flowers have all faded away, people's spiritual world seems to have found support.

六 说一说 (Ask and Answer)

1. 歌曲中的"层层风雨"和"云开日出"各借指什么？
2. "四君子"是指哪四种植物？
3. 为什么一些人建议将"梅花"选为中国的国花？
4. 为什么竹子象征着谦虚的品德？

学唱中国歌

七 做一做 (Tasks)

1. 你知道"岁寒三友"是指哪三种植物吗?
2. "爱我所爱"中的"所"是什么意思?你请举出汉语里其他"所"字结构的词。

八 词语链接 (Related Words or Phrases)

1. 欣赏	（动）	xīnshǎng	appreciate
2. 严冬	（名）	yándōng	severe winter
3. 来临	（动）	láilín	draw near
4. 凋谢	（动）	diāoxiè	wither
5. 不惧严寒		bú jù yánhán	not afraid of the severe cold
6. 不畏霜雪		bú wèi shāngxuě	not afraid of frost or snow
7. 歌颂	（动）	gēsòng	to sing praise of something
8. 呼啸	（动）	hūxiào	howl, roar
9. 君子	（名）	jūnzǐ	gentleman
10. 寄托	（动）	jìtuō	to place hopes and dreams on something

学唱中国歌

16 心太软
Too Soft a Heart

一 推荐絮语 (Introduction)

《心太软》(小虫作词作曲)曾经风靡一时,至今仍广为传唱。这首歌旋律简单,歌词也平白如话,但却说出了恋爱中痴情男女的痛苦、无奈、执著和挣扎。

歌声中我们好像看到一个"为伊消得人憔悴"、"衣带渐宽终不悔"的痴情人,也看到一个朋友对她的心疼和埋怨。也许正因为如此,这首歌才打动了无数的听众。

This song (lyrics and music by Xiao Chong) once swept China, and is still popular today. With its simple melody and plain oral language lyrics, it successfully expressed the painfulness, helplessness, persistence and struggle of men and women madly in love.

In the song, we can see an image of a lover, who is, like in the ancient poem, "My belt grows loose but I do not regret", "I'm pale and worn, but that person is worth it!" We can also see her friend feeling sorry for her and blaming her for being so blind. Maybe that is just why this song was so popular.

学唱中国歌

二 歌词对读 (Chinese and English lyrics)

nǐ zǒng shì xīn tài ruǎn xīn tài ruǎn
你总是心太软心太软，
You have such a soft soft heart,

dú zì yī gè rén liú lèi dào tiān liàng
独自一个人流泪到天亮。
Crying alone until the morning comes.

nǐ wú yuàn wú huǐ de ài zhe nà gè rén
你无怨无悔地爱着那个人，
You love that person with no complaint or regret,

wǒ zhī dào nǐ gēn běn méi nà me jiān qiáng
我知道你根本没那么坚强。
But I know you are just not that tough.

nǐ zǒng shì xīn tài ruǎn xīn tài ruǎn
你总是心太软心太软，
You have a soft soft heart,

bǎ suǒ yǒu wèn tí dōu zì jǐ káng
把所有问题都自己扛。
Taking all the troubles and taking it too hard.

xiāng ài zǒng shì jiǎn dān xiāng chǔ tài nán
相爱总是简单相处太难，
It's easy to fall but difficult to remain in love,

bú shì nǐ de jiù bié zài miǎn qiáng
不是你的就别再勉强。
If it's not yours, why would you not give it up.

yè shēn le nǐ hái bù xiǎng shuì
夜深了你还不想睡，
It's late in the night but you do not want to sleep,

nǐ hái zài xiǎng zhe tā ma
你还在想着他吗？
Are you still thinking about him?

nǐ zhè yàng chī qíng dào dǐ lèi bu lèi
你这样痴情到底累不累？
Don't you feel tired to be so blindly in love?

学唱中国歌

míng zhī tā bú huì huí lái ān wèi 明知他不会回来安慰。	When clearly you know he is not coming back.
zhǐ bú guò xiǎng hǎo hāo ài yī gè rén 只不过想好好爱一个人，	I know you just want to give sincere love to someone,
kě xī tā wú fǎ gěi nǐ mǎn fēn 可惜他无法给你满分。	But he could not give you a full mark.
duō yú de xī shēng tā bù dǒng xīn téng 多余的牺牲他不懂心疼，	The sacrifice you make he will not appreciate,
nǐ yīng gāi bú huì zhǐ xiǎng zuò gè hǎo rén 你应该不会只想做个好人。	And you should want more than just being a nice person.
o suàn le ba 哦，算了吧，	Come on, give it up,
jiù zhè yàng wàng le ba 就这样忘了吧。	Forget it as it is.
gāi fàng jiù fàng zài xiǎng yě méi yǒu yòng 该放就放，再想也没有用，	Let it go if nothing is going to help,
shǎ shǎ děng dài tā yě bú huì huí lái 傻傻等待他也不会回来，	Waiting like a fool but he's not turning his head,
nǐ zǒng gāi wèi zì jǐ xiǎng xiǎng wèi lái 你总该为自己想想未来。	Think about your own future, you blind woman.

学唱中国歌

三 生词详解 (New words)

1.	太	（副）	tài	too
2.	软	（形）	ruǎn	soft
3.	总是	（副）	zǒngshì	always
4.	独自	（副）	dúzì	alone
5.	流泪	（动）	liúlèi	shed tears
6.	天亮		tiānliàng	day break
7.	知道	（动）	zhīdào	know
8.	根本	（副）	gēnběn	at all
9.	那么	（副）	nàme	so
10.	坚强	（形）	jiānqiáng	tough
11.	把	（介）	bǎ	a marker for object
12.	所有	（形、名）	suǒyǒu	all
13.	问题	（名）	wèntí	problem
14.	都	（副）	dōu	all, entirely
15.	自己	（代）	zìjǐ	self
16.	扛	（动）	káng	shoulder
17.	相爱	（动）	xiāng'ài	love each other
18.	简单	（形）	jiǎndān	simple
19.	相处	（动）	xiāngchǔ	get along
20.	难	（形）	nán	difficult
21.	别	（副）	bié	do not
22.	再	（副）	zài	go on doing
23.	勉强	（动、形）	miǎnqiǎng	force someone to do something
24.	夜深		yèshēn	deep night

学唱中国歌

25.	睡	（动）	shuì	sleep
26.	这样	（代）	zhèyàng	this
27.	痴情	（动）	chīqíng	blindly love
28.	到底	（副）	dàodǐ	indeed
29.	累	（形）	lèi	tired
30.	明知	（动）	míngzhī	know clearly
31.	安慰	（动）	ānwèi	comfort
32.	可惜	（形）	kěxī	pity
33.	无法	（动）	wúfǎ	be unable to
34.	满分	（名）	mǎnfēn	full mark
35.	多余	（形）	duōyú	redundant
36.	牺牲	（动）	xīshēng	sacrifice
37.	懂	（动）	dǒng	understand
38.	心疼	（动）	xīnténg	feel sorry for, make one's heart ache
39.	应该	（动）	yīnggāi	should
40.	算了		suànle	let it be
41.	傻	（形）	shǎ	stupid
42.	等待	（动）	děngdài	wait
43.	未来	（名）	wèilái	future

学唱中国歌

四 歌曲欣赏 (Music sheet)

心太软

学唱中国歌

学唱中国歌

五 读一读 (Read the Following Passage)

知 音 Zhiyin

"知音"本来是"通晓音乐"的意思,用来借指"知己",与中国古代《列子·汤问》中的一个故事有关。

春秋时,楚国有个叫俞伯牙的人,精通音律,能弹一手好琴,把大自然的美妙融进了琴声,但是无人能听懂他的音乐,因此他感到十分孤独寂寞。一天,俞伯牙乘船游玩儿,美丽的景色激起了他的灵感,于是他弹起琴来。忽然俞伯牙感觉到有人在听他弹琴,抬头一看,只见一个樵夫站在岸边。樵夫名叫钟子期。他请钟

学唱中国歌

子期上船，为他弹奏。当他弹奏起赞美高山的曲调时，钟子期说："雄伟而挺拔，好像高耸入云的泰山一样！"当他弹奏起表现波涛奔腾的曲调时，钟子期又说："宽广浩荡，好像眼前滚滚的流水、无边的大海一样！"伯牙激动地说：你才是真的知音啊。两个人由于共同的爱好而成为了好朋友。

不久钟子期生病去世了，俞伯牙知道后，在钟子期的坟前弹奏了平生最后一支曲子，然后摔碎古琴，从此不再演奏。"俞伯牙摔琴谢知音"被传为千古佳话，自此以后，人们就开始把"知己"称作"知音"。世上如俞伯牙与钟子期这样的知音实在是太少了，那种知音难觅、知己难寻的故事在世世代代上演着。

Zhiyin literally means "understanding music" and is an equivalent to "soul mate", which originates from an old story recorded in *Lie Zi*: *Tang Wen* (a Taoist text).

In the period of Spring and Autumn, Yu Boya, a man in the kingdom of Chu, was an excellent musician, who knew how to play the *qin* (a Chinese string instrument). He composed his music with the feelings he received from the beautiful scenery of nature. But, unfortunately, nobody could understand his music. He felt really upset about it. One day, Boya took a trip on the river and the nice view evoked his feelings, so he began to play. Then, suddenly, Boya felt that someone was listening to his music. When he raised his head, he saw a woodcutter. The man was Zhong Ziqi. Boya invited Ziqi onto his boat and played for him. When Boya played a tune appreciating the high mountains, Ziqi would say, "How towering! Just like the Mount Tai!" When Boya played about the flowing water, Ziqi would say, "Vast and wide, just like a running river and the vast ocean!" Boya was so excited and said,

学唱中国歌

"You are the one who really understands my music!" Because of that, the two became great friends.

But soon after that, Ziqi fell ill and died. When Boya knew about this, he played his last tune in front of Ziqi's grave. Then he broke his *qin* and never played again. The story of how "Boya Broke the *Qin* in Return for the Friendship of His *Zhiyin*" is known as a famous story about friendship. From then on, people refer to their "soul mates" as their "zhiyin". In real life, friends like Boya and Ziqi are very rare. What we find more often are stories of searching for one's *zhiyin* but not succeeding.

六 说一说 (Ask and Answer)

1. 歌曲中"把所有问题都自己扛"是指什么？
2. 为什么说"不是你的就别再勉强"？
3. 你同意"相爱总是简单相处太难"这种观点吗？
4. "知音"本来的意思是什么？为什么可以用来指"知己"？

七 做一做 (Tasks)

1. "心太软"中的"太"表达了说话人什么样的感情？这里"太"的意思与"你的头发太长了"、"这场球踢得太棒了"里的"太"表达的感情一样吗？能不能把"心太软"换成"心很软"？
2. 你知道中国的古琴是什么样的？请查找资料说明。

学唱中国歌

八 词语链接 (Related Words or Phrases)

1. 风靡一时		fēngmí yī shí	being popular at one time
2. 至今	（副）	zhìjīn	up to now
3. 执著	（形）	zhízhuó	persisting
4. 挣扎	（动）	zhēngzhá	struggle
5. 憔悴	（形）	qiáocuì	waste away
6. 埋怨	（动）	mányuàn	complain
7. 知音	（名）	zhīyīn	bosom friend
8. 知己	（名）	zhījǐ	soul mate
9. 精通	（动）	jīngtōng	to be proficient in
10. 弹奏	（动）	tánzòu	play (usu. a string or keyboard instrument)

学唱中国歌

17 回娘家

Going Back to My Parents' Home

一 推荐絮语 (Introduction)

《回娘家》是一首河北民歌,但"回娘家"这种习俗并不只限于河北省,在中国从南到北的大部分地区都存在着。它特指结婚后住在夫家的女人回到自己原来的家看望父母。因为嫁到夫家后和自己父母见面的机会不多,所以回娘家常常是女人们盼望的日子。当喜气洋洋的《回娘家》唱响的时候,我们仿佛看到了打扮得漂漂亮亮的小媳妇,听到了她喜悦、兴奋的心跳声。

This is a folk song from the Hebei province, but the custom of "visiting the parents' home" is a common custom of Chinese people from the south to the north. Young women, after they get married, will go back to their parents' home for visits. When the daughter gets married, she does not have as much time as before to spend with her parents, so a married woman usually look forward to her trip home. When we hear this delightful song, we can see a dressed-up young lady and can hear her happy and excited heartbeat.

二 歌词对读 (Chinese and English lyrics)

fēng chuī zhe yáng liǔ ma　shuā lā　lā　lā　lā　lā
风吹着杨柳嘛,唰啦啦啦啦啦, Wind is blowing the willow,
(Sha-la-la-la-la)

学唱中国歌

<u>xiǎo hé lǐ shuǐ liú ma huā lā lā lā lā lā</u>
小河里水流嘛,哗啦啦啦啦啦,

<u>shuí jiā de xí fu tā zǒu ya zǒu de máng ya</u>
谁家的媳妇,她走呀走得忙呀,

<u>yuán lái tā yào huí niáng jiā</u>
原来她要回娘家,

<u>shēn chuān dà hóng ǎo</u>
身穿大红袄,

<u>tóu dài yī zhī huā</u>
头戴一枝花,

<u>yān zhi hé xiāng fěn tā de liǎn shàng chá</u>
胭脂和香粉她的脸上搽。

<u>zuǒ shǒu yī zhī jī</u>
左手一只鸡,

<u>yòu shǒu yī zhī yā</u>
右手一只鸭,

<u>shēn shàng hái bēi zhe yī gè pàng wá wá ya</u>
身上还背着一个胖娃娃呀,

<u>yī ya yī dé ér wèi</u>
咿呀咿得儿喂!

<u>yī piàn wū yún lái</u>
一片乌云来,

<u>yī zhèn fēng ér guā</u>
一阵风儿刮,

<u>yǎn kàn zhe shān zhōng jiù yào bǎ yǔ xià</u>
眼看着山中就要把雨下。

Water is flowing in the brook, (Hua-la-la-la-la)

A young women is walking in a hurry,

She is on her way to her parents' home,

Dressed in a bright red coat,

With a fresh flower in her hair,

Powder and blush on her face,

A chicken in the left hand,

A duck in the right hand,

On her back there is a plump baby, (Yi-ya-yi-der-way)

Here comes a dark cloud,

And there blows a sudden wind,

It is going to rain in the mountain.

学唱中国歌

<duǒ yòu méi chù duǒ>
躲又没处躲，

<cáng yòu méi chù cáng>
藏又没处藏，

<dòu dà de yǔ diǎn wǎng wǒ shēn shàng>
豆大的雨点往我身上

<dǎ ya yī ya yī dé ér wèi>
打呀，咿呀咿得儿喂！

There is nothing to shelter her,

And nowhere to hide,

Raindrops are falling on her body, (Yi-ya-yi-der-sway)

<lín shī le dà hóng ǎo>
淋湿了大红袄，

<chuī luò le yī zhī huā>
吹落了一枝花，

<yān zhī hé huā fěn biàn chéng hóng ní bā>
胭脂和花粉变成红泥巴。

The bright red clothes get wet,

The wind blows off the flower,

The blush and powder now becomes red mud,

<fēi le yī zhī jī>
飞了一只鸡，

<pǎo le yī zhī yā>
跑了一只鸭，

<xià huài le bèi hòu de xiǎo wá wa ya>
吓坏了背后的小娃娃呀，

<yī ya yī dé ér wèi>
咿呀咿得儿喂

<āi yo wǒ zěn me qù jiàn wǒ de mā>
哎哟，我怎么去见我的妈。

Flies away the chicken,

Runs away the duck,

Scared is the baby on the back,

(Yi-ya-yi-der-way)

Ah! How am I going to see my mum?

三 生词详解 (New words)

1. 娘家　　（名）　　niángjia　　mother's home
2. 杨柳　　（名）　　yángliǔ　　willow

学唱中国歌

3.	嘛	（助）	ma	*ma* (particle)
4.	唰啦	（拟声）	shuālā	*shua la* (sound of wind)
5.	哗啦	（拟声）	huālā	*hua la* (sound of water)
6.	媳妇	（名）	xífu	wife, daughter in law
7.	走得忙		zǒu de máng	walk in a hurry
8.	原来	（副、名）	yuánlái	as it turns out
9.	身	（名）	shēn	body
10.	穿	（动）	chuān	wear
11.	袄	（名）	ǎo	coat, top
12.	枝	（量）	zhī	measure word for flower
13.	胭脂	（名）	yānzhi	blush
14.	香粉	（名）	xiāngfěn	fragrant powder
15.	搽	（动）	chá	rub
16.	鸡	（名）	jī	chicken
17.	鸭	（名）	yā	duck
18.	背	（动）	bēi	carry on one's back
19.	胖	（形）	pàng	fat
20.	娃娃	（名）	wáwa	baby
21.	片	（量）	piàn	measure word for flower
22.	阵	（量）	zhèn	short period
23.	刮	（动）	guā	blow
24.	眼看	（名）	yǎnkàn	very soon
25.	处	（名）	chù	place
26.	豆大	（形）	dòudà	as big as a bean
27.	雨点	（名）	yǔdiǎn	raindrop
28.	往	（介）	wǎng	toward
29.	淋湿	（动）	línshī	wet from rain

学唱中国歌

30. 泥巴　　（名）　　　níba　　　　　mud
31. 飞　　　（动）　　　fēi　　　　　fly
32. 跑　　　（动）　　　pǎo　　　　　rain
33. 吓坏了　　　　　　　xià huài le　scare
34. 背后　　（名）　　　bèihòu　　　 behind the back
35. 哎哟　　（助）　　　āiyāo　　　　ow, ouch

四 歌曲欣赏 (Music sheet)

回娘家

风 吹 着 杨 柳 嘛, 刷 啦 啦 啦 啦, 小 河 里 水 流 嘛, 哗 啦 啦 啦 啦 啦, 谁 家 的

学唱中国歌

学唱中国歌

哎哟， 我怎么去见 我的 妈。

五 读一读 (Read the Following Passage)

回娘家 Visiting the Married Woman's Parents' Home

中国古代男尊女卑，妇女地位很低，出嫁从夫。民间谚语"嫁出去的姑娘泼出去的水"，意思就是指嫁出的女人是夫家的人了，要照顾好公婆和丈夫。因此婚后的女人不能总想着娘家，更不能无故回娘家。

但是渴望见到父母是人之常情，特别是在佳节到来、全家团圆的时候，所以在中国从南到北的很多地区都有特定的日子允许已婚的女子回家看望父母。这些日子虽然是约定俗成的，但在北方却大体一致，一般是农历正月初二。回娘家是一件很郑重的事，这一天女人一般都穿戴得整整齐齐，打扮得漂漂亮亮，由丈夫陪着，带着给父母和家人的礼物回去。因为女婿(也称姑爷)要陪同爱人一起回家看岳父岳母，因此在北方大部分地方，正月初二这一天也被称为"姑爷节"。

学唱中国歌

　　回娘家的日子并不只是在正月初二，在山东的一些地方是在正月初三，在陕西、河南等一些地方，也有六月六回娘家的习俗。

　　随着社会的进步，男女平等的思想已经深入人心，现在婚后女人回娘家已经不受任何限制，可以随时回家看自己的父母，但充满亲情的"姑爷节"却依然保留着。

　　In ancient China, women's social status was lower than men. Once they got married, they were supposed to follow and obey their husbands. A Chinese folk saying goes, "A married daughter is like spilled water", which means she now belongs to her husband and his family. Once a girl got married, she had the responsibility of taking care of the husband's family, so she was not to think about her own family too much. And most women could not visit their parents' home without a good reason.

　　Girls would surely miss their parents, especially when family members got together for a festival. In many areas of China, there were special days arranged for married women to visit their parents' homes. Though different areas may have different customs for the choosing of the day, in north China, that day fell on the second day of the lunar New Year. Women, accompanied by their husbands, would dress up and bring presents to their relatives. Because the son-in-law paid the visit too, in most areas of northern China, that day is referred to as "Guye Jie" (Son-in-law's Day).

　　In some parts of Shandong province, married women visited their parents' home on the second day after the lunar New Year's Day, while in Shanxi and Henan, women could also spend a day home on the 6th day of the 6th lunar month.

学唱中国歌

　　As society changes, men and women are now enjoying equal rights. Now married women do not have to follow any restrictions and can visit their parents as often as they wish, but the day full of family love, the "Guye Jie", is preserved.

六 说一说 (Ask and Answer)

1. 娘家是指什么？婆家呢？
2. 歌曲中的女人回娘家时怎样精心地打扮自己？
3. 回娘家时她带了哪些礼物？
4. 在你的国家,一年中有没有特定回娘家的日子？

七 做一做 (Tasks)

1. 用线段将左边词语与右边的解释连在一起

公公	妻子的父亲
婆婆	丈夫的母亲
丈人	女儿的丈夫
丈母娘	儿子的妻子
儿媳	父亲的姐妹
女婿	父亲的弟弟
姑姑	妻子的母亲
叔叔	丈夫的父亲

2. 介绍你的国家娘家与婆家的关系,并查找相关资料说明。

学唱中国歌

八 词语链接 (Related Words or Phrases)

1.	婆家	（名）	pójia	parents-in-law's home
2.	娶	（动）	qǔ	take a wife
3.	喜气洋洋		xǐqì yángyáng	jubilant
4.	男尊女卑		nán zūn nǚ bēi	Male is respectable while female is a weaker sex
5.	谚语	（名）	yànyǔ	proverb, saying
6.	人之常情	（名）	rén zhī chángqíng	human nature, natural and normal
7.	约定俗成		yuē dìng sú chéng	accepted through common practice
8.	郑重	（副）	zhèngzhòng	serious, solemn
9.	限制	（动、名）	xiànzhì	restrict, limit
10.	保留	（动）	bǎoliú	preserve

学唱中国歌

18 送 别

A Valediction

一 推荐絮语 (Introduction)

李叔同(弘一法师)是中国近代最富传奇色彩的人物之一。他出身豪门,自幼酷爱文学艺术,因擅长书法、绘画、音乐、篆刻而闻名中外。39岁时在杭州出家,法名演音,号弘一,后苦心修行成一代高僧,被尊为佛教律宗的第十一代传人。《送别》(奥德维作曲)的歌词是李叔同在日本留学时所作,词曲典雅、意境优美、弥漫着淡淡的伤感,一经传唱就受到海内外华人的广泛喜爱。

Li Shutong (or Master Hong Yi) is one of the most legendary figures in modern China's history. He was born to a wealthy family, and had a keen interest in literature and art. He was famous at home and aboard for his multiple talents in calligraphy, painting, music, and seal cutting. He was ordained as a monk in Hangzhou when he was 39, and was given the Buddhist names Yan Yin and Hong Yi, and later on he became the eleventh Dharma Master of Ritsu Sect. The lyrics of *A Valediction* (composed by J. P. Ordway) were written by Li while he was studying in Japan. The elegant combination of melody and lyrics created a refined artistic mood bathed in slight melancholy. Once it came out, it soon received the fancy of Chinese people both home and aboard.

学唱中国歌

二 歌词对读 (Chinese and English lyrics)

cháng tíng wài　gǔ dào biān
长亭外，古道边，　　　Beyond the distant pavilion, Beside the ancient road.

fāng cǎo bì lián tiān
芳草碧连天。　　　　　Jade green and fragrant, high grass joins the sky.

wǎn fēng fú liǔ dí shēng cán
晚风拂柳笛声残，　　　Evening breeze sways slanting willows, Dying flute notes linger still.

xī yáng shān wài shān
夕阳山外山。　　　　　On the hill behind the hill, the sun sets.

tiān zhī yá　dì zhī jiǎo
天之涯，地之角，　　　To the ends of the earth and corners of the seas,

zhī jiāo bàn líng luò
知交半零落。　　　　　Half our friends are scattered.

yī hú zhuó sǎ jìn yú huān
一壶浊洒尽余欢，　　　With a scoop of thick wine,

jīn xiāo bié mèng hán
今宵别梦寒。　　　　　Tonight's cold dreams shall be held at bay.

三 生词详解 (New words)

1. 长亭　　（名）　　chángtíng　　pavilion
2. 古道　　（名）　　gǔdào　　　　ancient road
3. 边　　　（名）　　biān　　　　　side
4. 芳草　　（名）　　fāngcǎo　　　grass

学唱中国歌

5.	碧	（名）	bì	green, jade-green
6.	连天		lián tiān	join the sky
7.	晚风	（名）	wǎnfēng	evening breeze
8.	拂	（动）	fú	softly touch
9.	笛声	（名）	díshēng	flute
10.	残	（形）	cán	broken, fragmented
11.	夕阳	（名）	xīyáng	setting sun
12.	之	（助）	zhī	of
13.	天涯	（名）	tiānyá	the end of earth
14.	地角	（名）	dìjiǎo	corner of the land
15.	知交	（名）	zhījiāo	friend
16.	半	（数）	bàn	half
17.	零落	（动、形）	língluò	scatter
18.	壶	（量、名）	hú	pot
19.	浊	（名）	zhuó	turbid
20.	酒	（名）	jiǔ	wine
21.	尽	（动）	jìn	exhaust
22.	余	（形）	yú	left
23.	欢	（名）	huān	joy
24.	今宵	（名）	jīnxiāo	tonight
25.	别	（动）	bié	be held at bay
26.	梦	（名）	mèng	dream
27.	寒	（形）	hán	cold

学唱中国歌

四 歌曲欣赏 (Music sheet)

送 别

长亭外，古道边，芳草碧连天。

晚风拂柳笛声残，夕阳山外山。

天之涯，地之角，知交半零落。

一壶浊酒尽余欢，今宵别梦寒。

长亭外，古道边，芳草碧连天。

晚风拂柳笛声残，夕阳山外山。

学唱中国歌

五 读一读 (Read the Following Passage)

中国诗歌 Chinese Poetry

在中国古代，配乐的韵文叫做"歌"，没有配乐的韵文称为"诗"。"诗"和"歌"像孪生兄弟一样亲密无间，所以人们总是把它们合在一起称作"诗歌"。

中国第一部诗歌总集《诗经》是两千五百年前问世的，分为《风》、《雅》、《颂》三类。《风》大都是民间诗歌，《雅》和《颂》是宴会的乐歌。这些歌曲都是先有音乐后填词的。后来，乐谱流失了，但歌词独立存在，一直流传下来。

汉代产生的"乐府"也是合于乐曲可以歌唱的诗。最初"乐府"并不指诗歌，而是指汉武帝建立的专门负责编制乐谱、搜集歌词的部门。到了魏晋六朝时，人们才将乐府所唱的诗简称为"乐府"。

唐代形成了近体诗，这种诗很讲究韵律。律是指语言运用有严格的规定。韵是韵脚，指诗句尾字主要韵母带发音相同或相近的音节。唐代还形成了另一种文体——词。它是合乐歌唱的，盛行于宋代，发展到元代成了散曲。词是一种新体诗，每个配乐唱歌的曲子都有曲牌，受一定的格律限制。

随着时代的变迁，新诗出现了。自由诗不好谱曲，所以诗与音乐的关系就逐渐疏远了。但是一些优秀作品还是讲究音乐美。因为新诗虽然没有严密的格式，但是有节奏，有丰富的感情和联想，语言简洁精炼，读起来就像唱歌一样。

In ancient China, *ge* referred to rhymed literature accompanied by music, and if the lines were not accompanied by music, they were referred to as *shi*. *Shi* and *ge* had a close relationship like twin brothers, therefore, people gave them a common name: *shige*.

学唱中国歌

The first collection of poems in China came 2,500 years ago. *Shi Jing* (Classic of Poetry) is divided into three parts: *Feng, Ya,* and *Song.* Most of *Feng* collections are folk songs, while *Ya* and *Song* are collections of songs sung at court banquets. These poems are words written for the already-existing music. Through history, the music sheets have been lost, but the lyrics remained.

Yue Fu in Han Dynasty were also poems used as lyrics. At the very beginning *Yuefu* referred to the governmental department established by Emperor Wu, the responsibility of which was composition of music and collection of lyrics.

Jintishi developed in Tang Dynasty was a strict form with rules governing the *yunlu* structure of a poem. *Yun* means rhyme, or the same or similar syllables at the endings of lines of verse. *Lu* means strict rules for language used in a poem. Another genre of poetry developed in Tang was *ci*. *Ci* refers to lyrics made up for existing tunes, which prospered in the Song Dynasty. *Ci* gradually developed into another form of lyrics in Yuan Dynasty, called *sanqu*. *Ci*, a genre of *Xintishi*, are sung with existing tunes and are required to fit into the meter and rhyme of the tune.

As time goes by, *Xinshi* (new poetry) appeared. Since it was difficult to find tunes to go with free verses, the relation between *shi* and music became aloof, but there are still excellent works which try to achieve the aesthetic effect of music. Though Xinshi does not have strict rules for structure, it has nice rhythm, rich emotion and imagination, and brief language, and one feels like singing when reading it out loud.

学唱中国歌

六 说一说 (Ask and Answer)

1. 你读过中国的古诗吗？和你熟悉的诗歌相比，你觉得中国的古诗有什么特点？
2. 你最喜欢的中国诗人是谁？你最喜欢的中国诗是哪一首？
3. 在你的国家送朋友去远方时会怎样告别？
4. 你还知道类似的诗或歌吗？

七 做一做 (Tasks)

1. "长亭"是"长的亭子"吗？请用一段话描绘一下歌中的景色。
2. 请搜集资料了解并介绍李叔同这个人物。

八 词语链接 (Related Words or Phrases)

1. 豪门	（名）	háomén	wealthy and influential family
2. 酷爱	（动）	kù'ài	to be very fond of, to ardently love
3. 擅长	（动）	shàncháng	to be good at
4. 闻名中外		wénmíng zhōngwài	be famous both in and outside China
5. 弥漫	（动）	mímàn	to fill the air, to pervade
6. 伤感	（名）	shānggǎn	melancholy
7. 孪生	（动）	luánshēng	to be born as twins
8. 亲密无间		qīnmì wú jiàn	being quite intimate
9. 脍炙人口		kuàizhì rénkǒu	to enjoy great popularity
10. 宴会	（名）	yànhuì	banquet

学唱中国歌

19 说唱脸谱
Rap Painting Mask

一 推荐絮语 (Introduction)

《说唱脸谱》(阎肃作词,姚明作曲)是一首将戏曲和西方说唱乐结合得很好的歌,具有东方传统戏曲的美感。歌曲延续了东西方乐风融合的精神,加入最具中华文化代表的传统戏曲——京剧与昆曲,将京剧优美的唱腔与西式 R&B 的唱腔巧妙地融合为一。这种巧妙的设计,使得听众心中有古典,耳中有新意!

Rap Painting Mask (lyrics by Yan Su, music by Yao Ming) is a song which combined elements of Chinese opera and western rap, and retained the aesthetic feelings of oriental traditional operas. The song extends the spirit of mixing eastern and western music styles, and added into it some characteristics of Peking Opera and Kun Opera. This clever design helps audience appreciate the aesthetic beauty of ancient art while enjoying modern rhythms in the ear.

二 歌词对读 (Chinese and English lyrics)

nà yī tiān yé ye lǐng wǒ qù bǎ jīng xì kàn
那一天爷爷领我去把京戏看, One day grandpa took me to the Peking Opera,

学唱中国歌

看见那舞台上面好多大花脸。

红白黄绿蓝颜色油的脸，

一边唱一边喊，

哇呀呀呀呀，

好像炸雷叽叽喳喳震响

在耳边。

蓝脸的窦尔敦盗御马，

红脸的关公战长沙，

黄脸的典韦白脸的曹操，

黑脸的张飞叫喳喳。

说实话京剧脸谱本来确实

挺好看，

I saw a lot of painted faces on the stage.

Faces painted in red, white, yellow, green, blue,

Chanting and shouting,

wa-ya-ya-ya,

Like noisy thunder roars

into my ears.

Dou Erdun, with a blue face, steals the emperor's horse,

Guan Gong, with a red face, fights in Changsha,

Dian Wei has a yellow face, and Cao Cao has a white one,

Zhang Fei, the black face, shouts "zha-zha-zha",

To be frank, the painted masks are not bad to look,

学唱中国歌

kě chàng de shuō de quán shì fāng yán
可唱的说的全是方言
zěn me tīng yě bu dǒng
怎么听也不懂，
màn man tēng tēng yī yī ya ya
慢慢腾腾咿咿呀呀
hēng shàng lǎo bàn tiān
哼 上老半天。

But the dialect they sing in is a bit hard to comprehend,
"yi-ya-", you have to wait a whole day for them to finish the long roar.

yuè duì bàn zòu yī tīng guāng shì
乐队伴奏一听光 是
luó gǔ jiā huo
锣鼓家伙，
lóng gè lī gè sān dà jiàn
咙个哩个三大件。

The instruments used in the band are gongs and drums,
"Long-ge-li-ge", the "three major ones".

zhè zěn me néng gòu gēn shàng shí dài
这怎么能够跟上时代
gǎn shàng cháo liú
赶上 潮流，
xī yǐn dāng dài xiǎo qīng nián
吸引当代小青年。

How could this catch up with the modern trend,
And attract the young guys.

zǐ sè de tiān wáng tuō bǎo tǎ
紫色的天王托宝塔，
lǜ sè de mó guǐ dòu yè chā
绿色的魔鬼斗夜叉，
jīn sè de hóu wáng yín sè de yāo guài
金色的猴王银色的妖怪，
huī sè de jīng líng xiào hā hā
灰色的精灵笑哈哈。

The purple Tian Wang has a pagoda in his hand,
The green devil fights with Yaksha,
Golden Monkey King and silver goblins,
Gray elves giggles "ha-ha".

学唱中国歌

<table>
<tr>
<td>

<ruby>我<rt>wǒ</rt></ruby> <ruby>爷爷<rt>yé ye</rt></ruby> <ruby>生气<rt>shēng qì</rt></ruby> <ruby>说<rt>shuō</rt></ruby> <ruby>我<rt>wǒ</rt></ruby> <ruby>纯粹<rt>chún cuì</rt></ruby> <ruby>这<rt>zhè</rt></ruby> <ruby>是<rt>shì</rt></ruby> <ruby>瞎捣乱<rt>xiā dǎo luàn</rt></ruby>，

<ruby>多<rt>duō</rt></ruby> <ruby>美<rt>měi</rt></ruby> <ruby>的<rt>de</rt></ruby> <ruby>精彩<rt>jīng cǎi</rt></ruby> <ruby>艺术<rt>yì shù</rt></ruby> <ruby>中华<rt>zhōng huá</rt></ruby> <ruby>瑰宝<rt>guī bǎo</rt></ruby>，

<ruby>就<rt>jiù</rt></ruby> <ruby>连<rt>lián</rt></ruby> <ruby>外国人<rt>wài guó rén</rt></ruby> <ruby>也<rt>yě</rt></ruby> <ruby>拍手<rt>pāi shǒu</rt></ruby> <ruby>叫好<rt>jiào hǎo</rt></ruby>，

<ruby>一个劲儿<rt>yī gè jìn ér</rt></ruby> <ruby>地<rt>de</rt></ruby> <ruby>来<rt>lái</rt></ruby> <ruby>称赞<rt>chēng zàn</rt></ruby>。

<ruby>生旦净末<rt>shēng dàn jìng mò</rt></ruby> <ruby>唱念作打<rt>chàng niàn zuò dǎ</rt></ruby> <ruby>手眼<rt>shǒu yǎn</rt></ruby> <ruby>身法<rt>shēn fǎ</rt></ruby> <ruby>功夫<rt>gōng fū</rt></ruby> <ruby>真是<rt>zhēn shì</rt></ruby> <ruby>不简单<rt>bù jiǎn dān</rt></ruby>，

<ruby>你<rt>nǐ</rt></ruby> <ruby>不懂<rt>bù dǒng</rt></ruby> <ruby>戏曲<rt>xì qǔ</rt></ruby> <ruby>胡说八道<rt>hú shuō bā dào</rt></ruby>，

<ruby>气<rt>qì</rt></ruby> <ruby>得<rt>de</rt></ruby> <ruby>爷爷<rt>yé ye</rt></ruby> <ruby>胡子<rt>hú zǐ</rt></ruby> <ruby>直<rt>zhí</rt></ruby> <ruby>往<rt>wǎng</rt></ruby> <ruby>脸上<rt>liǎn shàng</rt></ruby> <ruby>翻<rt>fān</rt></ruby>。

<ruby>老爷爷<rt>lǎo yé ye</rt></ruby> <ruby>你<rt>nǐ</rt></ruby> <ruby>别<rt>bié</rt></ruby> <ruby>生气<rt>shēng qì</rt></ruby>，

<ruby>允许<rt>yǔn xǔ</rt></ruby> <ruby>我<rt>wǒ</rt></ruby> <ruby>分辨<rt>fēn biàn</rt></ruby>。

<ruby>就算<rt>jiù suàn</rt></ruby> <ruby>是<rt>shì</rt></ruby> <ruby>山珍海味<rt>shān zhēn hǎi wèi</rt></ruby> <ruby>老<rt>lǎo</rt></ruby> <ruby>吃<rt>chī</rt></ruby> <ruby>也<rt>yě</rt></ruby> <ruby>会<rt>huì</rt></ruby> <ruby>烦<rt>fán</rt></ruby>，

</td>
<td>

Grandpa got mad and said I was deliberately making trouble,

The great treasures of delicate Chinese art,

Even foreigners applauded,

and said their praise.

The Kongfu of singing and performing are not that simple,

How can you judge what you don't understand,

With anger grandpa's beard was blown upon the face.

Don't be mad at me, dear grandpa,

Let me state my part.

One gets bored eating the same, even the most delicious, food every day,

</td>
</tr>
</table>

学唱中国歌

<small>yì shù yǔ shí dài bù néng lí tài yuǎn</small>
艺术与时代不能离太远，　　Art that's become obsolete,

<small>yào chuàng xīn yào fā zhǎn　　wā ya ya</small>
要创新要发展。（哇呀呀）　　Should make new changes and find new way. (Wa-ya-ya)

<small>ràng nà lǎo de shào de nán de nǚ de</small>
让那老的少的男的女的　　So that it could attract old,

<small>dà jiā dōu ài kàn</small>
大家都爱看，　　young, men, women-everyone,

<small>mín zú yí chǎn yī dài yī dài wǎng xià chuán</small>
民族遗产一代一代往下传。　　National relics, pass it on to the next generation.

<small>yī fú fú xiān míng de yuān yāng wǎ</small>
一幅幅鲜明的鸳鸯瓦，　　Pieces of smart Chinese-duck tiles,

<small>yī qún qún shēng dòng de huó pú sa</small>
一群群生动的活菩萨，　　Faces of vivid Buddha,

<small>yī bǐ bǐ gōu miáo yī diǎn diǎn kuā dà</small>
一笔笔勾描一点点夸大，　　Painted and exaggerated with strokes of brush,

<small>yī zhāng zhāng liǎn pǔ měi jiā jiā</small>
一张张脸谱美佳佳。　　Painted faces in opera, two thumbs up!

<small>wā hā hā</small>
（哇哈哈）

三 生词详解 (New words)

1. 爷爷　（名）　　yéye　　grandpa
2. 京戏　（名）　　jīngxì　　Peking Opera
3. 舞台　（名）　　wǔtái　　stage
4. 好多　（数）　　hǎoduō　　many

学唱中国歌

5. 花脸	（名）	huāliǎn	painted face
6. 颜色	（名）	yánsè	colour
7. 油	（动、名）	yóu	paint; oil
8. 喊	（动）	hǎn	shout, roar
9. 炸雷	（名）	zhàléi	frighteningly loud thunder
10. 叽叽喳喳		jījī zhāzhā	twitter
11. 震响		zhènxiǎng	make a loud sound
12. 说实话		shuō shíhuà	to tell the truth
13. 脸谱	（名）	liǎnpǔ	painted face
14. 本来	（副）	běnlái	originally
15. 确实	（副）	quèshí	indeed
16. 挺	（副）	tǐng	rather
17. 好看	（形）	hǎokàn	good-looking
18. 方言	（名）	fāngyán	dialect
19. 慢慢腾腾		mànmantēngtēng	slow
20. 哼	（动）	hēng	hum
21. 老半天	（名）	lǎobàntiān	for a rather long time
22. 乐队	（名）	yuèduì	band
23. 伴奏	（动）	bànzòu	accompaniment
24. 光	（副）	guāng	just
25. 锣鼓	（名）	luógǔ	gongs and drums
26. 家伙	（名）	jiāhuo	tool
27. 时代	（名）	shídài	times
28. 潮流	（名）	cháoliú	trend
29. 吸引	（动）	xīyǐn	attract
30. 当代	（名）	dāngdài	the present age
31. 青年	（名）	qīngnián	young people

学唱中国歌

32.	天王	（名）	tiānwáng	emperor in heaven
33.	宝塔	（名）	bǎotǎ	pagoda
34.	魔鬼	（名）	móguǐ	devil
35.	斗	（动）	dòu	fight with
36.	夜叉	（名）	yèchā	yaksha
37.	猴王	（名）	hóuwáng	Monkey King
38.	妖怪	（名）	yāoguài	goblin
39.	精灵	（名）	jīnglíng	elf
40.	笑哈哈		xiàohāhā	Laugh with a "ha-ha" sound
41.	纯粹	（形）	chúncuì	pure
42.	瞎	（形）	xiā	to no purpose
43.	捣乱	（动）	dǎoluàn	make trouble
44.	精彩	（形）	jīngcǎi	splendid
45.	艺术	（名）	yìshù	art
46.	中华	（名）	Zhōnghuá	China
47.	瑰宝	（名）	guībǎo	treasure
48.	连…也…		lián... yě...	even...
49.	外国人	（名）	wàiguórén	foreigner
50.	拍手叫好		pāishǒu jiàohǎo	clap hands and cheer
51.	一个劲儿		yīgèjìnr	continuously
52.	称赞	（动）	chēngzàn	praise
53.	戏曲	（名）	xìqǔ	Chinese opera
54.	胡说八道		hú shuō bā dào	to talk nonsense
55.	胡子	（名）	húzi	beard
56.	翻	（动）	fān	turn over
57.	允许	（动）	yǔnxǔ	allow
58.	分辨	（动）	fēnbiàn	distinguish

学唱中国歌

59.	就算	jiùsuàn	even
60.	山珍海味	shān zhēn hǎi wèi	delicacies from land and sea
61.	烦　　（形、动）	fán	annoy
62.	创新　　（动）	chuàngxīn	initiate
63.	发展　　（动）	fāzhǎn	develop
64.	民族　　（名）	mínzú	national
65.	遗产　　（名）	yíchǎn	relic
66.	一代　　（名）	yīdài	one generation
67.	鸳鸯瓦　（名）	yuānyāngwǎ	Chinese-duck-shaped roof tile
68.	生动　　（形）	shēngdòng	vivid
69.	菩萨　　（名）	púsa	Buddha
70.	勾描　　（动）	gōumiáo	draw the outline of
71.	夸大　　（动）	kuādà	exaggerate

四 歌曲欣赏 (Music sheet)

说唱脸谱

那一天爷爷领我去把京戏看，

看见那舞台上面好多大花脸。

学唱中国歌

学唱中国歌

(rap)说实话京剧脸谱本来确实挺好看,
(rap)我爷爷生气说我纯粹这是瞎捣乱,

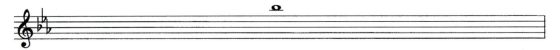

可唱的说的全是方言怎么听也不懂,慢慢腾腾咿咿呀呀哼上老半天。
多美的精彩艺术中华瑰宝,就连外国人也拍手叫好,一个劲儿地来称赞。

乐队伴奏一听光是锣鼓家伙 咙个哩个三大件。
生旦净末唱念作打手眼身法功夫真是不简单,

这怎么能够跟上时代赶上潮流,吸引当代小青年。
你不懂戏曲胡说八道,气得爷爷胡子直往脸上翻。

老爷爷 你 别 生 气,允 许 我 分 辩。

就算是山珍海味 老吃也会烦,

艺术 与 时 代 不能 离太远, 要 创 新 要 发 展

学唱中国歌

哇呀 呀 让那老的少的 男的女的 大家

都 爱看， 民族遗产一代一代 往下 传。

五 读一读 (Read the Following Passage)

京剧和脸谱 Peking Opera and Painted Face

在我国戏曲中，京剧是最具有全国性、典型性的剧种，它的剧目最丰富，表演最精细，流行最广泛，观众最普遍，影响也最大。因此，很多人称京剧为国粹。

虽然京剧的得名与北京有关，但并不是北京土生土长的戏曲。说起它的诞生，还要追溯到200多年以前。1790年，安徽的戏班先后进京献艺，获得空前成功。这样一种以徽调"二簧"和汉调"西皮"为主、兼收昆曲、秦腔、梆子和其他一些地方小调的精华，又结合了北京的语言特点，融化、演变而成的新剧种诞生了，这就是京剧。

由于北京是全国政治、文化的中心，所以自京剧诞生以后，就在全国范围内广泛流行，并逐渐传播到国外。在200多年的发展历程中，京剧在唱词、念白及字韵上越来越北京化，使用的二胡、京胡等乐器，也融合了多个民族的发明，逐渐走向成熟。

在演员的脸上涂上某种颜色以象征这个人的性格、品质、角色以及命运是京剧的一大特点，也是理解剧情的关键。简单地

学唱中国歌

讲，红脸含有褒义，代表忠勇者；黑脸为中性，代表猛智者；蓝脸和绿脸也为中性，代表草莽英雄；黄脸和白脸含贬义，代表凶诈者；金脸和银脸是神秘，代表神妖。

除颜色之外，脸谱的勾画形式也具有类似的象征意义。例如象征凶毒的粉脸，有满脸都白的粉脸，有只涂鼻梁眼窝的粉脸，面积的大小和部位的不同，标志着阴险狡诈的程度不同，一般说来，面积越大就越狠毒。总之，颜色代表性格，而不同的勾画法则表示性格的程度。脸谱起源于上古时期的宗教和舞蹈面具，今天许多中国地方戏中都保留了这种传统。

Among the Chinese operas, Peking Opera is the nationally influential and the most typical one. Its repertoire includes the largest number of works. The performance skills are the most developed, and it has the largest audience and is the most influential opera in China. Many people call it "the cream of Chinese culture".

Though "Peking" is in its name, Peking Opera originated somewhere else. It was born over 210 years ago, when, in the year 1790, opera troupes from Anhui Province came to Beijing and made great success. The music of the opera consists of two major types of melodies: *Erhuang* from Anhui and *Xipi* originated from Shanxi, and at the same time it also took in music elements from tunes from other sources like Kun Opera, Qin Opera and Bangzi, etc. The dialect of Beijing is used in the performance. And gradually, the blending of a new type of opera, the Peking Opera, was born.

Developed in the political and cultural center, Peking Opera soon claimed nationwide popularity and even spread to areas outside China. In the past 200 years of development, Peking became more and more local in both singing, reciting, and rhyming. The

学唱中国歌

instruments used in the band (like *erhu* and *jinghu*) also matured by taking in ideas from people of other ethnic groups.

One of Peking Opera's characteristics has some performers' faces painted to reveal personality, character, and fate in the story. To understand the story, one can get clues from the pattern and coloring of the painted faces. Easily recognizable examples of coloring include red, a positive color denoting uprightness and loyalty, black, a neutral color representing forcefulness and intelligence, yellow or white, negative colors given to the evil or crafty characters, and mysterious colors like gold or silver, which are painted on the faces of gods or spirits.

Besides colors, the patterns of the painted faces also have similar symbolic meanings. Paints in different areas of different size denote different degrees of that special character that color resembles. For example, the white color could be painted all over the face, or only on the nose and eyes, which reveals different degrees of craftiness and evilness. Generally speaking, larger painted areas reflect more severe characteristics. All in all, colors resemble personality, and the pattern reveals how big a part that characteristic takes in his entire personality. The painted faces originated from early ancient times in religious and dancing masks. In many local operas of China, this tradition can still be seen today.

六 说一说 (Ask and Answer)

1. 你看过京剧吗？感觉怎么样？
2. 歌曲中爷爷和"我"对京剧的看法有什么不同？

学唱中国歌

3. 京剧的脸谱有什么特点？试着猜猜下面哪一个是坏人？
4. 在你的国家有类似京剧这样的艺术形式吗？

七 做一做 (Tasks)

1. 歌里唱的"锣鼓家伙"、"咙个哩个三大件"指的是什么？你知道京剧里还用哪些乐器伴奏？
2. 介绍中国的京剧"生旦净末丑"等，并查找相关资料说明。

八 词语链接 (Related Words or Phrases)

1. 丰富	（形）	fēngfù	rich
2. 广泛	（形）	guǎngfàn	broad
3. 普遍	（形）	pǔbiàn	common
4. 国粹	（名）	guócuì	the quintessence of Chinese culture
5. 诞生	（动）	dànshēng	naissance
6. 精华	（名）	jīnghuá	distillate
7. 成熟	（形）	chéngshú	mature
8. 关键	（名）	guānjiàn	key
9. 褒义	（名）	bāoyì	with positive meaning
10. 贬义	（名）	biǎnyì	with negative meaning

学唱中国歌

Vocabulary

A

阿娇	Ā jiāo	10
啊	a	2
哎哟	āiyāo	17
爱	ài	3
爱情	àiqíng	8
爱人	àirén	6
爱我所爱	ài wǒ suǒ ài	15
安慰	ānwèi	16
袄	ǎo	17
傲立	àolì	15

B

把	bǎ	16
把握	bǎwò	13
爸爸	bàba	11
白色	báisè	3
百合花	bǎihéhuā	7
半	bàn	18
伴奏	bànzòu	19
包容	bāoróng	9
褒义	bāoyì	19
宝塔	bǎotǎ	19
保留	bǎoliú	17
背	bēi	17
背后	bèihòu	17
奔	bèn	11
奔驰	bēnchí	3
本来	běnlái	19
鼻子	bízi	4
碧	bì	18
避风	bìfēng	14
边	biān	18
贬义	biǎnyì	19
变	biàn	8
变幻莫测	biànhuàn mòcè	13
辫子	biànzi	5
别	bié	16
别	bié	18
别人	biérén	5
波涛	bōtāo	14
菠萝	bōluó	5
脖子	bózi	4
不惧严寒	bú jù yánhán	15
不客气	búkèqi	2
不能	bùnéng	12
不畏霜雪	bú wèi shuāngxuě	15
不用谢	búyòngxiè	2

C

才	cái	8
彩虹	cǎihóng	14
残	cán	18
苍茫	cāngmáng	15
藏躲	cángduǒ	14
操心	cāo xīn	11
草莓	cǎoméi	5
草原	cǎoyuán	3
层层	céngcéng	15
搽	chá	17
长	cháng	4
长寿	chángshòu	1
长亭	chángtíng	18
常	cháng	11

141

学唱中国歌

唱	chàng	10
潮流	cháoliú	19
称赞	chēngzàn	19
成熟	chéngshú	19
痴情	chīqíng	16
充满	chōngmǎn	10
惆怅	chóuchàng	10
愁	chóu	6
处	chù	17
处世哲学	chǔshì zhéxué	9
穿	chuān	17
穿透	chuāntòu	10
船	chuán	10
创新	chuàngxīn	19
吹	chuī	1
锤	chuí	11
纯粹	chúncuì	19
此	cǐ	15
脆弱	cuìruò	9
村庄	cūnzhuāng	10
挫折	cuòzhé	14

D

达坂城	Dábǎn Chéng	5
打动	dǎdòng	11
大	dà	5
大家好	dàjiā hǎo	2
大雁	dàyàn	8
带	dài	5
但	dàn	8
诞生	dànshēng	19
蛋糕	dàngāo	1
当代	dāngdài	19
捣乱	dǎoluàn	19
到底	dàodǐ	16
的	de	2
灯塔	dēngtǎ	14

等待	děngdài	16
等候	děnghòu	14
笛声	díshēng	18
地角	dìjiǎo	18
点	diǎn	1
凋谢	diāoxiè	15
跌倒	diēdǎo	14
懂	dǒng	16
都	dōu	16
斗	dòu	19
豆大	dòudà	17
独自	dúzì	16
对不起	duìbuqǐ	2
多余	duōyú	16
朵	duǒ	7

E

耳朵	ěrduo	4

F

发展	fāzhǎn	19
翻	fān	19
烦	fán	19
烦恼	fánnǎo	9
饭	fàn	11
方言	fāngyán	19
芳草	fāngcǎo	18
仿佛	fǎngfú	12
仿制	fǎngzhì	13
放弃	fàngqì	14
飞	fēi	17
分辨	fēnbiàn	13
分辩	fēnbiàn	19
分担	fēndān	14
芬芳	fēnfāng	7
纷扰	fēnrǎo	13
粉红色	fěnhóngsè	3

学唱中国歌

丰富	fēngfù	19	国粹	guócuì	19
风	fēng	10			
风靡一时	fēngmí yī shí	16		**H**	
风雨	fēngyǔ	14	孩子	háizi	11
夫妻	fūqī	6	海拔	hǎibá	12
拂	fú	18	寒	hán	18
浮现	fúxiàn	10	喊	hǎn	19
			豪门	háomén	18
	G		好	hǎo	2
盖头	gàitou	4	好多	hǎoduō	19
干燥	gānzào	12	好看	hǎokàn	19
港口	gǎngkǒu	14	好像	hǎoxiàng	4
高亢	gāokàng	12	何时	héshí	8
高楼	gāolóu	6	河水	héshuǐ	10
歌	gē	12	荷花	héhuā	7
歌颂	gēsòng	15	黑色	hēisè	3
歌谣	gēyáo	10	哼	hēng	19
个	gè	2	红色	hóngsè	3
给	gěi	5	猴王	hóuwáng	19
根本	gēnběn	16	后背	hòubèi	11
跟	gēn	11	呼唤	hūhuàn	12
工作	gōngzuò	11	呼啸	hūxiào	15
共鸣	gòngmíng	11	胡说八道	hú shuō bā dào	19
贡献	gòngxiàn	11	胡子	húzi	19
勾描	gōumiáo	19	壶	hú	18
姑娘	gūniang	3	湖水	húshuǐ	3
古道	gǔdào	18	糊里糊涂	húlihútu	9
古老	gǔlǎo	10	糊涂	hútu	9
故乡	gùxiāng	10	花开花落	huā kāi huā luò	13
刮	guā	17	花脸	huāliǎn	19
关键	guānjiàn	19	哗啦	huālā	17
关心	guānxīn	9	欢	huān	18
光	guāng	19	欢叫	huānjiào	8
广泛	guǎngfàn	19	欢乐	huānlè	6
广阔	guǎngkuò	15	欢颜	huānyán	13
归来	guīlái	6	还	hái	3
瑰宝	guībǎo	19	黄色	huángsè	3

学唱中国歌

灰色	huīsè	3
回	huí	11
回忆	huíyì	10
会	huì	8
慧眼	huìyǎn	13
活泼	huópō	11

J

叽叽喳喳	jījī zhāzhā	19
鸡	jī	17
吉祥	jíxiáng	6
几	jǐ	6
几分	jǐ fēn	9
季节	jìjié	13
寄托	jìtuō	15
佳节	jiājié	6
家	jiā	3
家	jiā	6
家伙	jiāhuo	19
假	jiǎ	13
嫁	jià	5
嫁妆	jiàzhuang	5
坚持	jiānchí	14
坚强	jiānqiáng	16
肩	jiān	11
剪	jiǎn	15
简单	jiǎndān	16
鉴定	jiàndìng	13
将	jiāng	7
接受	jiēshòu	14
街头	jiētóu	6
洁白	jiébái	3
斤斤计较	jīnjīn jìjiào	9
今宵	jīnxiāo	18
金色	jīnsè	3
尽	jìn	18
京戏	jīngxì	19

精彩	jīngcǎi	19
精华	jīnghuá	19
精灵	jīnglíng	19
精明	jīngmíng	9
精髓	jīngsuǐ	11
精通	jīngtōng	16
敬礼	jìng lǐ	2
静悄悄	jìngqiāoqiāo	8
九州	Jiǔzhōu	6
久久	jiǔjiǔ	12
酒	jiǔ	18
就算	jiùsuàn	19
菊花	júhuā	7
橘子	júzi	5
橘子	júzi	5
句	jù	13
聚	jù	6
眷恋	juànliàn	12
觉得	juéde	8
君子	jūnzǐ	15
骏马	jùnmǎ	3

K

坎坷	kǎnkě	14
看透	kàntòu	14
扛	káng	16
可	kě	12
可惜	kěxī	16
渴望	kěwàng	11
空闲	kòngxián	11
孔雀	kǒngquè	8
苦	kǔ	14
酷爱	kù'ài	18
夸	kuā	7
夸大	kuādà	19
快乐	kuàilè	1
脍炙人口	kuàizhì rénkǒu	18

学唱中国歌

筷子	kuàizi	11	埋怨	mányuàn	16
			满	mǎn	7
			满分	mǎnfēn	16
L			慢慢腾腾	mànmantēngtēng	19
蜡烛	làzhú	1	漫长	màncháng	14
来	lái	5	猫头鹰	māotóuyīng	8
来临	láilín	15	没关系	méi guānxi	2
兰花	lánhuā	7	玫瑰	méigui	7
蓝	lán	3	眉	méi	4
唠叨	láodao	11	梅花	méihuā	7
老半天	lǎobàntiān	19	美德	měidé	11
老鹰	lǎoyīng	8	美酒	měijiǔ	6
乐队	yuèduì	19	妹妹	mèimei	5
累	lèi	16	朦胧	ménglóng	10
梨	lí	5	梦	mèng	18
连…也…	lián... yě...	19	梦幻	mènghuàn	12
连天	lián tiān	18	弥漫	mímàn	18
脸	liǎn	4	迷雾	míwù	14
脸颊	liǎnjiá	4	勉强	miǎnqiǎng	16
脸谱	liǎnpǔ	19	面积	miànjī	12
临摹	línmó	13	面条	miàntiáo	1
淋湿	línshī	17	民族	mínzú	19
零落	língluò	18	明白	míngbái	13
领	lǐng	5	明亮	míngliàng	4
留下	liúxià	12	明知	míngzhī	16
流	liú	10	模仿	mófǎng	13
流浪	liúlàng	6	魔鬼	móguǐ	19
流泪	liúlèi	16	茉莉花	mòlìhuā	7
流落	liúluò	6	牡丹	mǔdan	7
绿	lǜ	3	幕	mù	9
孪生	luánshēng	18			
锣鼓	luógǔ	19	**N**		
			那	nà	4
M			那里	nàlǐ	5
妈妈	māma	11	那么	nàme	16
麻雀	máquè	8	男尊女卑	nán zūn nǚ bēi	17
马车	mǎchē	5	难	nán	16
嘛	ma	17			

145

学唱中国歌

难道	nándào	12
难得	nándé	9
难免	nánmiǎn	14
脑海	nǎohǎi	10
泥巴	níba	17
你	nǐ	1
你好	nǐ hǎo	2
你们好	nǐmen hǎo	2
娘家	niángjia	17
鸟	niǎo	8
您好	nín hǎo	2
宁愿	nìngyuàn	14
柠檬	níngméng	5
凝结	níngjié	13
农历	nónglì	6

P

拍手叫好	pāishǒu jiàohǎo	19
旁边	pángbiān	10
胖	pàng	17
跑	pǎo	17
陪同	péitóng	11
朋友	péngyou	2
片	piàn	17
平	píng	5
平安	píng'ān	6
平均	píngjūn	12
苹果	píngguǒ	4
婆家	pójia	17
菩萨	púsa	19
葡萄	pútao	5
普遍	pǔbiàn	19

Q

祈盼	qípàn	12
起(来)	qǐ(lái)	4
谦让	qiānràng	9

前额	qián'é	4
桥	qiáo	10
憔悴	qiáocuì	16
亲密无间	qīnmì wú jiàn	18
亲热	qīnrè	13
亲人	qīnrén	6
勤劳	qínláo	12
青	qīng	3
青藏高原	Qīng-Zàng gāoyuán	12
青年	qīngnián	19
轻松	qīngsōng	11
清楚	qīngchu	13
情丝	qíngsī	13
晴空	qíngkōng	14
庆祝	qìngzhù	1
秋波	qiūbō	4
秋天	qiūtiān	4
曲调	qǔdiào	10
娶	qǔ	17
却	què	8
确实	quèshí	19

R

让	ràng	4
热乎	rèhu	9
人间	rénjiān	9
人烟稀少	rényān xīshǎo	12
人之常情	rén zhī chángqíng	17
日夜	rìyè	12
容易	róngyì	11
揉	róu	11
如果	rúguǒ	5
如今	rújīn	8
软	ruǎn	16

S

涩	sè	9

学唱中国歌

傻	shǎ	16
山川	shānchuān	12
山珍海味	shān zhēn hǎi wèi	19
擅长	shàncháng	18
伤感	shānggǎn	18
舌头	shétou	4
身	shēn	17
生动	shēngdòng	19
生活	shēnghuó	11
生活化	shēnghuóhuà	11
生日	shēngrì	1
胜利	shènglì	14
什么	shénme	8
石榴	shíliu	5
石路	shílù	5
时代	shídài	19
时间	shíjiān	11
世界	shìjiè	13
事情	shìqing	11
柿子	shìzi	5
是	shì	2
树	shù	8
树梢	shùshāo	4
刷	shuā	11
唰啦	shuālā	17
谁	shuí	12
水仙	shuǐxiān	7
睡	shuì	16
说实话	shuō shíhuà	19
思念	sīniàn	6
思乡	sīxiāng	10
酸楚	suānchǔ	9
算了	suànle	16
随	suí	10
岁月匆匆	suìyuè cōngcōng	10
所有	suǒyǒu	16

T

太	tài	16
谈	tán	11
弹奏	tánzòu	16
淌	tǎng	10
涛	tāo	13
桃子	táozi	5
体贴	tǐtiē	13
天鹅	tiān'é	8
天空	tiānkōng	3
天亮	tiānliàng	16
天堂	tiāntáng	3
天王	tiānwáng	19
天涯	tiānyá	18
甜	tián	5
跳	tiào	8
停	tíng	8
挺	tǐng	19
童年	tóngnián	10
头发	tóufa	4
图	tú	11
团圆	tuányuán	6
退缩	tuìsuō	14
托起	tuōqǐ	9

W

娃娃	wáwa	17
外国人	wàiguórén	19
外头	wàitou	6
弯	wān	4
晚风	wǎnfēng	18
碗	wǎn	11
万丈	wànzhàng	15
往	wǎng	17
往日	wǎngrì	9
往事	wǎngshì	10
忘掉	wàngdiào	9

学唱中国歌

忘怀	wànghuái	12
望	wàng	13
为	wèi	11
惟妙惟肖	wéi miào wéi xiào	13
未必	wèibì	13
未来	wèilái	16
伪造	wěizào	13
温存	wēncún	9
温度	wēndù	9
文物	wénwù	13
闻名中外	wénmíng zhōngwài	18
问题	wèntí	16
我	wǒ	2
握手	wò shǒu	2
乌云	wūyún	14
无法	wúfǎ	16
无奈	wúnài	14
无情	wúqíng	13
无言	wúyán	12
无怨无悔	wú yuàn wú huǐ	15
舞台	wǔtái	19
雾	wù	13

X

夕阳	xīyáng	18
西瓜	xīguā	5
吸引	xīyǐn	19
牺牲	xīshēng	16
习俗	xísú	1
媳妇	xífu	17
洗	xǐ	11
喜	xǐ	14
喜气洋洋	xǐqì yángyáng	17
喜鹊	xǐquè	8
喜悦	xǐyuè	14
戏曲	xìqǔ	19
细	xì	4
瞎	xiā	19
下面	xiàmian	10
吓坏了	xià huài le	17
掀	xiān	4
限制	xiànzhì	17
相爱	xiāng'ài	16
相处	xiāngchǔ	16
相连	xiānglián	12
香	xiāng	7
香粉	xiāngfěn	17
向	xiàng	8
啸啸	xiāoxiāo	15
孝	xiào	11
笑哈哈	xiàohāhā	19
笑容	xiàoróng	11
笑语	xiàoyǔ	13
谢谢	xièxie	2
心	xīn	8
心疼	xīnténg	16
欣赏	xīnshǎng	15
汹涌	xiōngyǒng	14
胸膛	xiōngtáng	10
许愿	xǔ yuàn	1
旋律	xuánlǜ	12

Y

呀	ya	2
鸭	yā	17
牙齿	yáchǐ	4
胭脂	yānzhi	17
淹没	yānmò	15
严冬	yándōng	15
颜色	yánsè	19
眼	yǎn	4
眼睛	yǎnjing	4
眼看	yǎnkàn	17
宴会	yànhuì	18

148

学唱中国歌

谚语	yànyǔ	17
燕子	yànzi	8
赝品	yànpǐn	13
羊群	yángqún	3
杨柳	yángliǔ	17
妖怪	yāoguài	19
摇	yáo	10
摇曳多姿	yáoyè duōzī	13
遥望	yáowàng	12
遥远	yáoyuǎn	10
要	yào	5
爷爷	yéye	19
夜叉	yèchā	19
夜空	yèkōng	10
夜深	yèshēn	16
一	yī	2
一般样	yībānyàn	4
一代	yīdài	19
一定	yīdìng	5
一个劲儿	yīgèjìnr	19
伊人	yīrén	15
遗产	yíchǎn	19
已经	yǐjīng	8
以假乱真	yǐ jiǎ luàn zhēn	13
艺术	yìshù	19
意念	yìniàn	9
因为	yīnwèi	8
银色	yínsè	3
引起	yǐnqǐ	11
饮	yǐn	6
应该	yīnggāi	16
樱桃	yīngtáo	4
鹦鹉	yīngwǔ	8
硬	yìng	5
永久	yǒngjiǔ	12
勇敢	yǒnggǎn	14
优美	yōuměi	10

忧	yōu	14
忧伤	yōushāng	10
悠悠	yōuyōu	10
油	yóu	19
有	yǒu	3
又	yòu	4
余	yú	18
雨点	yǔdiǎn	17
郁金香	yùjīnxiāng	7
鸳鸯	yuānyang	8
鸳鸯瓦	yuānyāngwǎ	19
原来	yuánlái	17
圆	yuán	4
远古	yuǎngǔ	12
约定俗成	yuē dìng sú chéng	17
月饼	yuèbing	6
月儿	yuè'ér	6
月季	yuèjì	7
月亮	yuèliàng	4
允许	yǔnxǔ	19

Z

再	zài	16
再见	zàijiàn	2
在	zài	6
赞美	zànměi	12
藏族	Zàngzú	12
炸雷	zhàléi	19
摘	zhāi	7
绽放	zhànfàng	15
张罗	zhāngluo	11
找	zhǎo	2
找到	zhǎodào	2
照	zhào	6
哲理	zhélǐ	14
这	zhè	3
这样	zhèyàng	16

149

学唱中国歌

阵	zhèn	17	主人公	zhǔréngōng	10
珍惜	zhēnxī	14	祝	zhù	1
真迹	zhēnjì	13	祝福	zhùfú	1
真切	zhēnqiè	13	庄严	zhuāngyán	12
真情	zhēnqíng	15	庄严	zhuāngyán	12
真挚	zhēnzhì	9	装糊涂	zhuāng hútu	9
震响	zhènxiǎng	19	准备	zhǔnbèi	11
挣扎	zhēngzhá	16	桌	zhuō	11
郑重	zhèngzhòng	17	浊	zhuó	18
之	zhī	18	着	zhe	5
枝	zhī	17	紫色	zǐsè	3
枝桠	zhīyā	7	自己	zìjǐ	16
知道	zhīdào	16	自由	zìyóu	14
知己	zhījǐ	16	总是	zǒngshì	16
知交	zhījiāo	18	棕色	zōngsè	3
知音	zhīyīn	16	走得忙	zǒu de máng	17
执著	zhízhuó	16	阻隔	zǔgé	15
只	zhi	5	嘴	zuǐ	4
只	zhi	5	嘴唇	zuǐchún	4
至今	zhìjīn	16	左右	zuǒyòu	14
至理名言	zhìlǐ míngyán	9	座	zuò	12
中华	Zhōnghuá	19	做	zuò	11
中秋节	Zhōngqiūjié	6			